101 Creative Worship Ideas for Children's Church

by Jolene Roehlkepartain

Group®

Loveland, Colorado

DEDICATION

To Claire Ashley, Krystine Barnes, Caitlyn Batzlaff, Jeff Grignon, Molly Holte, Matthew Huang, Sarah Jones, Charlie Liedl, Jeffrey Medema, Jonathan Mitchell, Derek Powers, Micah Roehlkepartain, Kathryn Schmidt, Lyda Sou, Matthew Steinbergs, Katie Taintor, Laura Teich, and Elizabeth Turnbull of St. Luke Presbyterian Church in Wayzata, Minnesota, for making worship more active, meaningful, and memorable.

101 Creative Worship Ideas for Children's Church
Copyright © 1995 Jolene Roehlkepartain

Credits
Book Acquisitions Editor: Mike Nappa
Editors: Beth Rowland Wolf, Christine Yount, and Candace McMahan
Senior Editor: Paul Woods
Creative Products Director: Joani Schultz
Copy Editor: Ann Carr
Art Director: Helen Lannis
Cover Art Director: Liz Howe
Computer Graphic Artist: Kari Monson
Production Manager: Gingar Kunkel

Unless otherwise noted, Scriptures quoted from The Youth Bible, New Century Version, copyright © 1991 by Word Publishing, Dallas, Texas 75039. Used by permission.

Library of Congress Cataloging-in-Publication Data
Roehlkepartain, Jolene L., 1962-
    101 creative worship ideas for children's church / by Jolene Roehlkepartain.
      p.   cm.
    Includes indexes.
    ISBN 1-55945-601-9
    1. Worship (Religious education) I. Title.
    BV1522.R64 1995
    264'.0083--dc20
                                   95-13912
                                   CIP

10 9   04 03 02 01
Printed in the United States of America.

Visit our Web site: www.grouppublishing.com

CONTENTS

95835

SECTION 3: CHILDREN'S WORSHIP SERVICES

THE WONDER OF CHILDREN AND WORSHIP

Too often we think children and worship don't mix. But this opinion shows we define worship too narrowly, and in the process, we make worship inaccessible for children. As adults, we think worship is an opportunity to be quiet—to listen and be reverent and still before God. Sometimes worship *is* quiet. However, sometimes it's equally appropriate to be exuberantly and noisily joyful when we worship.

This book will expand your definition of worship and broaden the horizons of your worship experience. You'll find prayers, Scriptures, devotions, messages, object lessons, offerings, music, and creative movement—all elements of worship. When you look closely at these sections, you'll notice that most of them require children to *not* sit still and to *not* be quiet. In essence, the ideas in this book will encourage children to worship God with their wiggles and enthusiasm.

To create a worship experience that children will truly get involved in, try these tips:

● **Rethink your idea of worship.** Yes, people can worship God with silence, but what about shouts of praise and creative wiggles?

● **Make worship age-appropriate.** Since children are naturally active, their worship should also be active. Keep in mind that children can appreciate quiet and reverent worship *if* they're also given the opportunity to move and use their "outside voices" every so often.

● **Mix and match worship elements.** Start off by using the five complete worship services in Section 3. Then when you feel ready to create your own worship for children, mix and match the prayers, Scriptures, creative movements, music, offerings, and object lessons in Section 1.

● **Plan, but be flexible.** Good experiences are planned, but the best experiences are ones that combine lots of planning with an openness to God's spirit. One adult co-worship leader became upset after leading a Palm Sunday worship service with the children. She overheard a 4-year-old asking her mom, "Did you know it's pompom Sunday?" The other worship leader was thrilled because she thought that captured the essence of Palm Sunday—the little girl thought of it as a celebration in which the participants are like cheerleaders at a football game. The following year, all the children were excited about Palm Sunday because that girl remembered how wonderful "pompom" Sunday was to her.

● **Use puppets.** We often forget the power of puppets. They often bring out the best in children in a way people can't. Children trust puppets because puppets are small like children and less threatening than adults. I've had better luck getting tough messages across with puppets than I have ever had with other methods.

● **Enjoy.** Worship does contain elements of repentance, but a lot of worship is meant to be enjoyed. Worship occurs whenever a community of Christians comes together to praise God. So as your community of children comes together, enjoy the time praising and worshiping God. You'll be surprised to see what happens. God works in wonderful ways.

SeCTioN 1: CReATiVe WoRsHiP iNGReDieNTs

The goal of children's worship is to help children express themselves to their Creator. In this section, you'll find seven ways to help children worship God:

- **Creative prayers**—Innovative ways for children to communicate with God.
- **Bible stories and Scripture readings**—Well-known and not-so-well-known Bible stories that'll help children learn more about God.
- **Children's messages**—Quick minisermons that involve children in discovering God's truth.
- **Object lessons**—Fresh ideas to help children connect with Bible principles.
- **Music ideas**—New songs to sing and fun ways to enjoy music.
- **Creative movement ideas**—Fun movements to help children use their wiggles to praise God.
- **Holiday ideas**—New ways to worship God that celebrate special days.

The ideas are simple to use. Just choose one or more ideas that best fit your group of children. Gather any needed supplies ahead of time. They'll be easy to find; just look around your home or the church building.

Follow the instructions step by step and with a prayerful attitude. Ask God to make God's presence evident in the worship activities. Without God's participation in worship, even the best worship activities become humdrum.

Be sure to explore the questions that are listed in many of the activities. Involve your group in discussions that will help solidify their beliefs and that will put a worshipful spirit into the activities.

Mix and match worship elements. Use the prayers, Scriptures, creative movements, music, and object lessons to create an entire worship service or just use one or two ideas to supplement an existing service for children.

However you incorporate these activities into your children's worship, the activities will help children experience the wonder and mystery of God. This is your opportunity to instill in children the idea that God is loving *and* fun-loving—and that our all-powerful God cares deeply about the prayers and worship of even the youngest child.

Use these ideas to help your children learn to enjoy their relationship with God. Then you can say together with the children, "I was happy when they said to me, 'Let's go to the Temple of the Lord' " (Psalm 122:1).

CHAPTER I

PRAYERS AND OFFERINGS

BUBBLE PRAYER

Have one person blow a bubble with bubble gum while the other children each quickly name something God has given to them or something God has done for them (pertaining to a certain theme) until the bubble pops. Choose themes such as school, home, friends, play time, church, mealtime, and chores. For example, if the theme is school, children may say that God has given them "good teachers" or "lunch time every day." When the bubble pops, have children clap, cheer, and call out, "Thank you, God." Then name another theme and have a different child blow a bubble while children take turns naming something to thank God for.

After several children have blown bubbles, pray: **God, you give us so many things. We thank you for...** Mention several of the children's ideas. **We want to praise you for your gifts to us.** Have the children cheer, "Thank you, God. Yea, God! Yea, God! Amen!"

POSITIVE REFLECTIONS

Do this prayer in a room with a large mirror, such as a bathroom. You could also have children pray this prayer using a window that shows their reflections.

Have the children line up in front of the mirror or window. Squirt an orange-sized ball of shaving cream on the mirror in front of each child. Have the children trace their images in the mirror, using the shaving cream.

As they're tracing, have children think about why they're thankful that God created them.

When the tracings are complete, have the children continue to stand so their reflections are inside their shaving cream tracings. Then have children pray, thanking God for the unique qualities God has given them.

Pray: **God, you have made each of us special and unique. No one else in the world is exactly like us. We're glad you created us. Amen.**

DEDICATION DELIGHT

Have children sit or stand in a circle. Give one child a 2- or 3-inch-wide roll of crepe paper. Have that child say how his or her life affects others, such as "My smile makes others happy" or "I help others when they're sad." When the child finishes, have the group say together, "Thank you, God, for this gift."

Then have the child hold on to the loose end of the crepe paper while passing the roll to the child next to him or her. Repeat the prayer until the crepe paper encompasses the entire circle.

Then pray: **God, we know that you want us to use the gifts you give us to help others. We can see that our gifts can be used to tie us together as your family, just as this crepe paper ties us together in one big circle. Help us to help and love each other every day. Amen.**

PENNY OFFERING

For this offering you'll need a penny for each child. If children have brought their own offerings, have them add them to the box at the end of the activity.

Have children form a circle, then put a box in the middle of the circle and give one child a penny. Say: **Pass the penny around the circle as quickly as you can. When I say, "Give it to God," the person holding the penny runs around the circle one time and then places the penny in the box in the middle of the circle while naming one thing he or she can give to God. For example, you might say, "God, I give you my time" or "God, I promise to give you praises every day."**

Say: **Go** and have the children start passing the coin. Then say: **Give it to God.** Have the child with the penny run around the circle, put the penny in the box, and say one thing he or she can give to God. Then start another penny around the circle. Make sure that each child gets a chance to go to the middle of the circle and give something to God.

After everyone has had a turn, have children join hands and raise them in the air. Then say: **God, please use our gifts to do good things.** Have children shout "amen!"

FORGIVENESS HUGS

Have children spread out in the room. Say: **I'm going to say a prayer asking God to forgive us when we do bad things. Every time I say, "Forgive us, God," run and find someone to hug and say, "God loves you." As I pray, walk around the room.**

Start the prayer. Make sure that all the children are receiving and giving hugs. Include statements such as these in your prayer:

God, sometimes we disobey.
Forgive us, God. (Pause.)
God, sometimes we hit.
Forgive us, God. (Pause.)
God, sometimes we lie.
Forgive us, God. (Pause.)
God, sometimes we pout.
Forgive us, God. (Pause.)
God, sometimes we don't cooperate.
Forgive us, God. (Pause.)
Amen.

A BIG HAND

Have children stand in a circle, then give one child a glove to wear. Say: **This prayer is a thank you prayer to God for making each person. The child wearing the glove must put the glove on the hand of the next person while saying, "Thank you, God, for making** (child's name)**." That child then does the same for the next person.**

Continue the prayer all the way around the circle.

After each child has worn the glove at least once, end the prayer by saying: **We want to give you a big hand, God, for making each one of us. Amen.** Have children clap to praise God.

BUBBLE GUM BURST

Give each child a piece of bubble gum. Have children blow bubbles and pop them every time you say "joyful noise" during the following prayer:

God, you give us a place to live that's warm and cozy.
We thank you, God, and make a joyful noise to you. (Pause while children blow bubbles and pop them.)
God, you care for us through our moms, dads, brothers, sisters, grandparents, and other family members.

We thank you, God, and make a joyful noise to you. (Pause while children blow bubbles and pop them.)

God, you give us good food to make us strong.

We thank you, God, and make a joyful noise to you. (Pause while children blow bubbles and pop them.)

God, you give us opportunities to learn more about you in church.

We thank you, God, and make a joyful noise to you. (Pause while children blow bubbles and pop them.)

God, you are the greatest!

We thank you, God, and make a joyful noise to you. (Pause while children blow bubbles and pop them.)

Amen.

PRAYER CHAINS

Give each child several 1×6-inch strips of paper. Have the children write prayer requests or draw pictures of prayer requests on the strips of paper. Then staple or tape the strips together in circles to create one long paper chain. Hang the paper chain from the ceiling or around a door.

TOE SQUEEZE

Use this prayer any time you'd like the children to pray sentence prayers.

Have children lie head to toe on their backs in a circle, holding onto the person's toes ahead of them. If it's summertime, this is a great prayer to do outside in the grass. Have the children look up at the ceiling or sky. Have one child start the prayer by either saying a sentence prayer aloud or praying silently, then saying, "Please hear my prayer, God." When each child finishes praying, have him or her squeeze the toes of the next child so that child knows to begin praying. After each child has had a turn, have children squeeze each other's toes at the same time and say "amen."

WHISPER PRAYERS

Have children surround a wooden cross. If a wooden cross is unavailable, draw a cross on a piece of tagboard and hang it up so that children can reach it.

Have the children take turns going to the cross and whispering a prayer to Jesus. They might want to confess a sin, make a special request that they'd be embarrassed to pray about out loud, or say thank you to Jesus for answering an earlier prayer.

When all the children have gone to the cross, pray: **Jesus, thanks for always listening to us. We praise you for always being there for us. Amen.**

Leave the cross in your worship center and encourage the children to use the cross as a reminder to pray often.

BODILY PRAISE

Have children skip around the room while you start this prayer. Explain that when you name a part of the body, children are to cluster as a big group and touch the part that was named with the corresponding part of their bodies. As soon as children do that, have them spread out and start skipping again until another part of the body is named.

For example, say: **We praise you, God, for making neat knees** (children touch their knees against other kids' knees), or **We praise you, God, for happy hips** (children touch their hips together).

Name parts of the body such as neat knees, awesome arms, handy hands, fantastic feet, super shoulders, excellent elbows, happy hips, beautiful backs, and eager ears.

To end the prayer, have the children stop and wiggle their entire bodies while you pray: **God, we are wonderfully made. And we praise you with all that we are. Amen.**

WORRIES AWAY

Put sand in a large, shallow box. Stand a candle for each child in the sand, then turn the room lights down low. Say: **God, sometimes we worry. We worry about school. We worry about what's happening at home. We worry about feeling left out. And when we worry, sometimes it feels like we're in a dark, lonely place. Please listen to our worries.**

Tell children to think about one worry they have and to pray silently to God about that worry. After children have prayed, light an extra candle and place it in the sand. Have children approach the candles one at a time and light a candle with the flame from the extra candle. Supervise children carefully—especially young ones. Once all the children have done this and all the candles are burning brightly, say: **God, you are our light in the darkness. You're bigger than our worries. We know we can trust you to conquer our worries and bring light into our lives. Amen.**

PULL TOGETHER

Have children sit in a circle facing one another and link arms. Instruct children to lean back and feel the pull of stretching away from each other each time you name a tough situation. When you name a way that God is good, have children pull inward and closer together.

Pray:

God, sometimes we don't want to go to school. (Children lean back and feel the pull of stretching away.)

But, God, we praise you for being with us wherever we are. (Children pull inward and close together.)

God, sometimes our friends say mean things to us. (Children lean back and feel the pull of stretching away.)

But, God, we praise you for your everlasting kindness. (Children pull inward and close together.)

God, sometimes we don't want to listen to our parents. (Children lean back and feel the pull of stretching away.)

But, God, we praise you for always loving us no matter what we do. (Children pull inward and close together.)

God, since we can't physically hug you, we'll hug each other. (Have the group stand up, put their arms around each other's waists, and squeeze in tight.)

Amen.

ALONE AND THEN TOGETHER

Lead this prayer while the children do the actions in parentheses. Start by having the children hold hands and stand in a circle.

God, sometimes we feel alone. (Drop hands.)

God, sometimes we feel small. (Squat down.)

God, sometimes we don't want you to see us. (Hide face in hands.)

But, God, you reach out to us. (Reach out and touch a person next to you.)

God, you help us feel tall. (Help the person to a standing position.)

God, we know you want us to worship and pray together. (Hold hands.)

God, we are your people and your followers. (Kneel while holding hands.)

Thank you, God. (Hold hands high in the air.)

Amen.

FLOWER OFFERINGS

Make arrangements to provide altar flowers for an adult worship service.

Bring enough daisies, carnations, wildflowers, or another inexpensive flower to give each child one flower. Also provide a vase with water in it.

Give each child one flower and ask all the children to think about one thing they can give to God. Have children each offer their gifts to God in a sentence prayer then put their flowers in the vase.

After all the children have prayed and put their flowers in the vase, have the children place the flower arrangement on the altar.

CHAPTER 2

BIBLE STORIES AND SCRIPTURE READINGS

THE ZACCHAEUS STRETCH

Theme: Jealousy

Scripture: Luke 19:1-10

Description: Have children try different ways to become tall, such as these:

- Stand on tiptoes.
- Stand on a chair.
- Give another child a piggyback ride.
- Make a pyramid.
- (Optional) Go outside and climb a tree.

Afterward, ask:

- **How does it feel to be small?**
- **What do you like about being small?**
- **What would you like about being tall?**
- **Would you rather be tall or small? Explain.**

Then read aloud the Scripture. Explain that Zacchaeus felt very small, but Jesus accepted Zacchaeus just as he was. Tell the children that God loves them just as they are, too.

ALL ALONE

Theme: Feeling left out

Scripture: Genesis 37:18-24

Description: Have children form a circle, hold hands, and skip together as they sing a favorite song. While the children are singing, call out a child's name. Have that child leave the circle and stand away from the group. Then quickly call another child's name. Have children who've been called out stand alone in different parts of the room. One by one, call out children to leave the circle until everyone has left the circle. Ask:

- **What was it like to have your name called?**
- **When do you feel left out in real life?**
- **What can you do when you feel left out?**

Read Genesis 37:18-24 aloud. Say: **Joseph felt left out, too. His brothers didn't like him much. He felt really alone when his brothers threw him into an empty well.** Ask:

- **What could Joseph have done to get along better with his brothers?**
- **If you had been one of Joseph's brothers, what could you have done to help Joseph get along better with his brothers?**
- **What can you do to help others who feel left out?**

Say: **All of us feel left out and alone sometimes. But we can help each other feel loved and accepted. Let's include everyone in our singing so that no member of our group feels alone.**

Have the children join hands and re-form the circle. Sing the song together again. Then have the children gently squeeze each other's hands to say, "I care for you."

PRAISE, PRAISE

Theme: Praise

Scripture: Psalm 148:1-5

Description: Form pairs. Give each pair an inflated balloon. Explain that when you begin reading the Scripture aloud, one child in each pair will throw the balloon into the air, and when you say the word "praise," the other child will hit the balloon. Once the balloon is in the air, have the partners take turns hitting the balloon each time you read the word "praise."

Read the Scripture aloud. Afterward, ask:

- **What can we praise God for?**
- **How do you feel when you praise God?**
- **Why does God want us to praise him?**

Say: **Our praise tells God that we love and appreciate God. Our God is a great God, and it's good to praise God every day.**

GROWING IN FAITH—TOGETHER

Theme: Christian growth

Scripture: Philemon 4-7

Description: Have children follow your actions as you read the Scripture.

Say: **"I always thank God** (cup your hands around your mouth and shout, "Thank you, God")

when I mention you (point one finger to your mouth and look up)

in my prayers (fold hands as if you're praying)**,**

because I hear (put your hand to your ear)

about the love you have for all God's holy people and the faith you have in the Lord Jesus. (Squeeze together for a group hug.)

I pray that the faith you share (hold hands)

may make you understand (nod your head)

every blessing we have in Christ. (Hold hands out as if you're getting something.)

I have great joy (jump up and shout, "We're happy")

and comfort (put your arms through another child's arms so that everyone is linked)**,**

my brother (hold someone's hand)**,**

because the love you have shown to God's people (fold your hands over your heart)

has refreshed them." (Fling your arms wide.)

Afterward, say the verses all the way through without the actions. Then ask:

● **Why do we pray for each other?**
● **Why do we thank God for other people?**
● **Why do we show love to each other?**
● **How do we learn about God from each other?**

Say: **God has given us one another to help us grow more like Jesus. We pray for each other, we do kind things for each other, and we learn about God from each other. All of these things help us grow in God.**

RememBeRiNG

Theme: Commandments

Scripture: Numbers 15:37-41

Description: Have each child make a belt out of blue yarn. An easy belt can be made by cutting a length of yarn that will go around a child's waist 12 times, then folding the yarn into 10 equal lengths and putting a knot in each end. Tie the belt around the child's waist.

Have the children cut small pieces of various colors of yarn to tie onto the blue belt to create a fringed effect. Read aloud the Scripture as children put on their belts. Discuss how the different colors can remind them of the different commandments.

Have children stand in a circle and hold hands. Then have children raise their hands and say, "We remember God's commandments. We remember God's commandments" as they walk to the left. Then repeat the activity with children walking to the right. Have the children sit down. Ask:

- ● **Why did God tell Moses to wear a belt like this?**
- ● **When did God tell Moses to wear the belt? Why?**
- ● **Why does God say it's important to obey all the commandments?**
- ● **How can we remember to obey the commandments?**

Say: **God's commandments are important. In biblical times people wore belts to remind them to obey God. Today we come to church to learn how to obey the commandments. Sometimes we put them on posters that we hang on our walls. God's commandments tell us how to please God. We can do our best to remember and obey them every day.**

Me! No, Me!

Theme: Arguing

Scripture: Mark 9:33-35

Description: Have each child find a partner. Tell children to argue with their partners. Have one child say, "I'm the best," while the other child insists, "No, I'm the best." Have the children continue to argue back and forth for a minute.

After a while, quiet the children. Read the Scripture aloud. Ask:

- ● **What was it like to argue?**
- ● **Who won? Explain.**
- ● **What did Jesus say about people who want to be the best?**
- ● **How can you be a servant?**
- ● **Why is it good to serve others instead of always trying to be the best?**

Have the children rejoin their partners. Have them shake hands with their partners and say, "I'll do my best to serve you."

Then say: **Jesus is the best example of a great person who served others. Jesus is God, but he came to earth to heal people and to help them. We can serve people every day, too. God will be pleased when we do our best to serve others.**

Being Christian

Theme: Being strong

Scripture: Ephesians 6:10, 14-18a

Description: Read the Scripture aloud as you lead the children in these actions:

"Finally, be strong in the Lord and in his great power. (Show the muscle in your arm.)

So stand strong, with the belt of truth tied around your waist (take a step and stand strong with arms and legs akimbo, then put on an imaginary belt)

and the protection of right living on your chest. (Put on an imaginary vest and hold your thumbs up.)

And on your feet wear the Good News of peace to help you stand strong. (Put on imaginary shoes and hold someone's hand to symbolize peace.)

And also use the shield of faith with which you can stop all the burning arrows of the Evil One. (Hold up an imaginary shield and duck behind it.)

Accept God's salvation as your helmet. (Put on an imaginary helmet.)

And take the sword of the Spirit, which is the word of God. (Hold up an imaginary sword.)

Pray in the Spirit at all times." (Fold hands in prayer.)

Have the children sit down. Ask:

● **Why does the Bible use the image of a soldier to tell us what it's like to be a Christian?**

● **Now that you've put on the armor of God, how do you feel?**

● **What are you ready to do?**

Say: **God's armor prepares us to live the Christian life. With God's armor we're ready to fight against Satan and against temptation. We're prepared to serve others and to please God, who is our commander in chief.**

TIME FOR EVERYTHING

Theme: Time

Scripture: Ecclesiastes 3:4-6

Description: Have children stand in a circle. Ask a volunteer to stand in the middle of the circle. Tell kids they are a large clock. Have the child in the middle stick out his or her arms to form the hands of the clock.

Read the Scripture aloud, one part at a time. After you read each part, have the child in the middle point his or her arms at two people. Those people must act out the line of Scripture according to the actions in parentheses.

"There is a time to cry (pretend to cry)

and a time to laugh. (Laugh.)

There is a time to be sad (look down at the floor)

and a time to dance. (Dance.)

There is a time to throw away stones (throw away an imaginary object)

and a time to gather them. (Pick up an imaginary object.)

There is a time to hug (hug yourself)

and a time not to hug. (Put arms down at your sides.)

There is a time to look for something (pretend to look for something)

and a time to stop looking for it. (Shrug shoulders and stop looking.)

There is a time to keep things (pretend to hold something)

and a time to throw things away." (Pretend to throw something away.)

Afterward, ask:

● **The Bible says there is a time for everything. When is it time to be sad?**

● **When is it time to dance?**

● **What would you think if someone danced during a sad time?**

● **What does it mean that there's a time for everything?**

Say: **God knows that some things make us sad and some things make us happy. God knows that sometimes we need to cry and sometimes we need to laugh. God understands how we feel.**

▲ ▲ ▲ ▲ ▲ ▲ ▲ ▲

LOVE NEVER ENDS

Theme: Love

Scripture: 1 Corinthians 13:4-8a

Description: Say: **I'm going to read from the Bible. Every time you hear the word "love," find someone to hold hands with. When you hear the word "love" again, let go of your partner's hand and find someone else to hold hands with.**

If you have an uneven number of children, allow one group of three each time.

After reading the Scripture aloud, repeat "Love never ends" four or five times. Ask:

● **What was it like to hold hands with a lot of different people?**

● **Why do you think the Bible talks about love so much?**

● **What does "Love never ends" mean?**

● **What makes people stop loving each other?**

● **How can God help you love others?**

Say: **The Bible says we should love each other because God loves us. Let's work hard to love everyone.**

ANOINTED ONES

Theme: Being chosen

Scripture: 1 Samuel 16:1, 11-13

Description: Have the children sit while you read the Scripture aloud.

Say: **God wanted to choose someone special to be the king. God looked at all the people in the land and chose David, a shepherd. David was so busy taking care of the sheep that the people had to go look for him. When they found David, Samuel anointed him with olive oil.**

Put a few drops of olive or vegetable oil in your hand. Let each child touch the oil and rub it between his or her fingers. Provide napkins for the children to wipe their hands. Ask:

● **What would it feel like to be anointed?**

● **How do you think David felt when Samuel anointed him to show he would be the next king?**

● **God told Samuel to anoint David to show that David was to be the next king. What do you think God might want you to do with your life?**

● **How do you think God will show you what you're supposed to do?**

Say: **God has a job for each one of us to do. David's job was to be the King of Israel. He worked hard to be a good king. We can each do our best to do a good job at whatever we've been chosen to do.**

GOD IS GREAT!

Theme: Praise

Scripture: Psalm 100

Description: Have children do the actions in parentheses as you read this Scripture aloud:

"Shout to the Lord, all the earth. (Make a joyful noise by shouting "hooray!")

Serve the Lord with joy (worship in glad ways by smiling and clapping)**; come before him with singing.** (Sing, "La, la, la, la.")

Know that the Lord is God. He made us, and we belong to him (hug yourself)**;**

we are his people, the sheep he tends. (Make sheep noises.)

Come into his city with songs of thanksgiving (have two children pair up and hold their hands up high while the other children walk through the "gate") and into his courtyards with songs of praise. (Praise God by holding hands in the air, shaking them, and saying, "Praise God!")

Thank him and praise his name. (Say, "Thank you, God.")

The Lord is good. His love is forever, and loyalty goes on and on." (Have children hug a friend. Then have pairs join up and hug. Then have foursomes join and hug. Continue until the whole group hugs.)

Ask:

- **Why is it important to praise God?**
- **How do you praise God at church? at home? at school?**
- **How often can we praise God?**

Say: **Praising God is important. It lets God know that we love God. It's fun, too. We can laugh and have a good time while we praise God. Praising God gives us joy.**

WIDE AND NARROW

Theme: Christian life

Scripture: Matthew 7:13-14

Description: Read aloud Matthew 7:13. Have children form two lines facing each other. Have the two lines stand as far apart as possible, forming a wide "path." Have one child walk down the path. Then let other children take turns walking down the path. Ask:

- **How easy was it to walk down this path?**

Read aloud Matthew 7:14. Have children form two lines facing each other. Have the two lines stand as close together as possible, forming a narrow path. Have one child walk down the path. Then let other children take turns walking down the path. Ask:

- **How easy was it to walk down this path?**
- **Which is easier: to walk down a narrow or a wide path?**
- **What does the Bible mean when it talks about the path to life?**
- **What makes the narrow way hard?**

Say: **The narrow way is hard because it means we don't do whatever we want to do. Being on the narrow way means that we live to please God and that we obey God. Sometimes that's hard. Sometimes we're tempted to displease God. But the narrow way is the path that leads to God. When we choose to travel on the narrow way, we'll be able to live with God forever.**

LOST AND FOUND

Theme: Celebration

Scripture: Luke 15:8-10

Description: Hide a penny for each child. Have children search for the coins. When a child finds a coin, have all the children come and form a circle around the child with the coin. Have the children hold hands, skip to the right, and say, "Hooray! Hooray! We found a penny today!"

Hold the coin in your hand for everyone to see while everyone who hasn't found a coin searches again. Repeat the celebration every time a coin is found. Once all the coins are found, ask:
- **How did you feel when you found a penny?**
- **Did you like celebrating each coin? Why or why not?**
- **Why do you think each coin was so important?**
Read aloud the Scripture. Then ask:
- **What did the woman do when she lost her coin?**
- **What did she do when she found her coin?**
- **How was our celebration like the way heaven celebrates when Jesus brings us into his family?**

Say: **Each one of us is as important to God as that coin was to the woman who lost it. We're important treasures. God rejoices when we decide to live for him. It makes God as happy as the woman was when she found the coin that had been lost.**

EASIER WALKING

Theme: Following God

Scripture: 1 John 1:5-10

Description: Have the group form a human chain in which children line up in front of each other and put a hand on the shoulder of the person in front of them. Give every fourth child a flashlight.

Have another adult stand at the front of the line and lead the children around the room as you read the Scripture aloud. Turn off the lights. If the room isn't dark, have the children walk with their eyes shut. Read the verses by flashlight. When you read, "If we walk in the light," have the children turn on the flashlights and open their eyes. Have the children continue walking until you've finished reading the Scripture. Then have the children sit down. Put away the flashlights and ask:
- **How hard was it to walk without light?**
- **How did turning on the flashlights help you see?**
- **What does it mean to walk in God's light?**
- **How does walking in God's light help us be closer to God?**
- **Why does the Bible say that God is light?**
Say: **When we walk in God's light, we walk in the way that pleases God and leads us to good things. When we walk in the darkness, we can get lost or hurt or involved in something bad. God is pleased when we choose to walk in the light of God's way.**

CHAPTER 3

CHILDREN'S MESSAGES

PHILIP AND THE ETHIOPIAN

Theme: Missions

Scripture: Acts 8:26-31

Description: Before children do this activity, write each of these words on a separate piece of paper: rauha, vrede, paich, miers, paci, udo, mir, frieden, kabayapaan, pax, rabo, aman, fred, sith, paci, pacea, paz, pace, mutende, and ramyde. Give each child one of these pieces of paper. Have children walk around the room and compare their words with other children's words. Then ask:

● **How different or similar was your word from the other children's words?**

● **What do the words mean?**

● **Have you ever heard people speaking in a language that you couldn't understand? How did it make you feel?**

Read the Scripture aloud. Tell how the Ethiopian was having a hard time understanding God's Word and that Philip taught him what it meant. Explain that when we meet people who are different from us, we tend to focus on the differences rather than the similarities. Tell children that the words on their papers can all be translated into the same English word: peace. Ask:

● **How are people who speak different languages different? How are they similar?**

● **How can we help people who speak other languages learn about Jesus?**

Say: **God created everything in our world. That means God created all of the different languages that people speak. People all over the world are different—they speak different languages, they have different customs, and they even look different. But everyone still needs to know about God. Just as Philip helped** the Ethiopian understand what the Bible says, we can help people in other countries learn about God, too.

GIVING SOMETHING NEW

Theme: Giving

Scripture: Luke 6:38

Description: Give each child a sticker. Tell the children to give their stickers to each other. The goal is to not have a sticker. But children have to take the stickers offered to them, and they can't give a sticker to someone who has just given them one.

After a while, read the Scripture aloud. Then ask:

● **How easy was it to get rid of your sticker?**
● **How did it feel to keep giving stickers away?**
● **How did it feel to keep receiving more stickers?**
● **What do you give others in real life?**
● **What are the rewards of giving to others in real life?**

Say: **When we give to others, we often find that we have more to give. We receive many rewards when we give to others—we feel good when we help others, and we become good friends when we care enough to give. But most important, we please God when we give to other people.**

Give each child a sticker to take home.

FOLLOW ME

Theme: Discipleship

Scripture: Matthew 4:18-22

Description: This game is similar to Duck, Duck, Goose. Have the children sit on the floor in a circle. Choose one child to be "It." Have It walk around the circle and tap each child lightly on the head and say, "Person, person, disciple." When It says, "disciple," have the child who was tapped jump up and link arms with It. Then have them continue the game, tapping the other children and saying, "Person, person, disciple." Each time a child is chosen, the players link arms so that eventually a long chain of players is formed. Play until all the children are part of the chain.

Then have the children sit down. Say: **Let's listen to what the Bible says about Jesus' choosing disciples.** Read Matthew 4:18-22. Then ask:

● **What is a disciple?**
● **Why do you think Jesus picked so many disciples?**
● **Why do you think he picked the people he picked?**
● **Why were disciples important?**

- **What made a person a disciple?**
- **How can we become modern-day disciples?**

Say: **Disciples are people who follow and obey a teacher. When Jesus asked Simon, Andrew, James, and John to follow him, they put down what they were working on and immediately started to follow Jesus. We, too, can be Jesus' disciples, or followers. You had great ideas on how to be a modern-day disciple. We can obey Jesus, we can serve others, and we can tell others about Jesus. When we do these things, we show that we're Jesus' disciples.**

REMOLDING

Theme: Hope

Scripture: Romans 9:21

Description: Have children make "pinch pots." Give each child a small ball of modeling dough or clay. Have each child push a finger into the middle of the ball and then squeeze and pinch the sides to make the walls thinner and taller. If you have time, give children toothpicks to scratch out designs in the clay. While the children are working, ask:

- **What will you put in your clay pot?**
- **If you were a potter who made things out of clay every day, what shapes would you make and what colors would you use?**

Say: **Listen to what the Bible says about making pottery.** Read the Scripture. Then say: **In this Bible verse the potter is God.** Ask:

- **What has God made?**
- **What has God created you to do?**
- **How is the way God makes us like the way we made the pots? How is it different?**

Say: **God made everything that we see. Everything God made has a purpose. We can be thankful to God for making us for a special purpose. Some of us made tall, narrow pots. Some of us made shallow, wide pots. It all depended on what we wanted to do with the pots. In the same way, God made us the way we are so we can accomplish the plan that God has for us.**

THE RED SEA

Theme: God's protection

Scripture: Exodus 14:1-25

Description: Say: **Listen to what the Bible says about the time the Eygptian army was chasing God's people.** Read the Scripture.

Then play Moses, Be Nimble. Choose three children to be the Egyptians, one child to be Moses, and the rest of the group to be the Israelites. Have the Israelites stand on one side of the room and the Egyptians stand on the opposite side of the room.

Have the Israelites call out this rhyme: "Moses, be nimble; Moses, let's flee! Stretch out your hand to open the sea!" Have Moses stretch out his or her hand as the Israelites try to crawl to the other side of the room without being tagged by an Egyptian. Have the Egyptians crawl, too, as they try to tag as many Israelites as they can.

When everyone has been caught or has made it to the other side, choose another child to be Moses and play again. Afterward, ask:

● **How did it feel to get tagged in this game?**
● **What happened to the Israelites in the story?**
● **How is being protected by God different from how we played this game?**
● **Tell about a time you needed God's protection in real life.**
● **How does God protect us?**

Say: **The Israelites were scared because it looked like they were trapped. They were right on the edge of the sea, and the Egyptian army was closing in on them. But God took care of them in a miraculous way. God opened the sea, and every one of them crossed safely to the other side. All of us need to be protected sometimes. Lots of scary things happen in life, but God promises to be with us and to take care of us just as God took care of the Israelites.**

WHO'S THERE?

Theme: Listening

Scripture: 1 Samuel 3:1-10

Description: Have everyone lie on the floor, then turn out the lights. Tap one child's shoulder and have him or her whisper another child's name. That child then asks, "Who's there?" The first child answers, "It's me." The second child must then guess who whispered his or her name. For example, tap Rachel's shoulder. Rachel whispers, "Hey, Michael." Michael replies, "Who's there?" Rachel says, "It's me." Then Michael has three chances to guess who called out his name.

After three unsuccessful guesses, the other children can guess. After someone guesses correctly, secretly choose another child to start the activity again. Continue until all the children have had a turn. Then read the Scripture aloud. Ask:

● **God spoke to Samuel in the middle of the night. How does God speak to us?**
● **How can you know when God talks to you?**

- **What can you learn by listening to God?**
- **Has God ever spoken to you? What did God say?**
- **What can we do to make sure we hear God when God speaks to us?**
- **What did Samuel do when he heard from God?**
- **What should we do when God speaks to us?**

Say: **God speaks to us in many ways. Sometimes we hear a still, small voice inside our hearts. Sometimes God speaks to us through the Bible. Sometimes God speaks to us through our parents or our teachers or through ministers. We need to listen very closely to hear what God says to us. And when we know that we've had a message from God, we need to be sure to obey it.**

PUSH, PULL

Theme: Cooperation

Scripture: Philippians 2:1-3

Description: Form pairs. Have partners kneel on the floor facing each other and sit on their heels. Have them put about eight inches of floor space between their knees and their partner's knees. Have partners grasp each other's arms at the elbows. Tell the pairs to lean back and pull on their partners' arms until their partners rise up on their knees. Ask:

- **Was it easy to get your partner to rise up on his or her knees? Why or why not?**
- **What would have made it easier?**

Say: **In this activity you were working against your partner. Listen to what the Bible says about working with others.** Read the Scripture aloud.

Say: **Now try the activity again. Take turns letting your partner gently pull you up.** Give the children a moment to do this. Then ask:

- **Why is it important to work together with other Christians?**
- **What can we accomplish when we work together?**
- **What can we do every day to work with others?**

Say: **As Christians, we all have the same goals: to follow God, to treat others with love, and to tell others about Jesus. We can help each other reach these goals by working together. We struggled when we worked against each other in this activity, but think how much we could accomplish if we combined all of our strength and our efforts!**

GOD'S SOLDIER

Theme: Christianity

Scripture: Ephesians 6:10-17

Description: Read the Scripture aloud. Ask:
- **Why did soldiers used to wear armor?**

Then form groups of four and have each group choose one person to dress up as "God's soldier." Provide aluminum foil, cardboard, gray yarn, tape, and scissors for the groups to work with. Have each group show its soldier to the rest of the class. Ask:
- **When we put on God's armor, what will we be protecting ourselves from?**
- **What will the belt of truth do for us?**
- **How will the protection of right living and the shield of faith protect us?**
- **Why should we wear the gospel of peace on our feet?**
- **Since we don't wear armor in the real world, how can we prepare ourselves to be God's soldiers?**
- **What will happen when we fight the enemy and win?**

Say: **The Bible says that we're fighting a spiritual war against evil. All of us know what it feels like to fight against the temptation to do wrong. That's what the spiritual war is like. We work to tell people about God, and we do our best to obey God and to please God. Sometimes it's hard because we're tempted to be selfish or to hurt others instead of helping them. But God gives us the tools we need—the armor—to fight temptation and to win over evil.**

TOO MUCH?

Theme: Materialism

Scripture: Luke 12:13-21

Description: Give one child the contents of a large bag of bite-sized candy bars (without the bag). Have the child try to keep all of the candy from the rest of the children as they try to get some. Tell the children not to hurt the child with the candy. Then say: **Let's see what the Bible says about the things we own.** Read the Scripture aloud. Ask:
- **What's it like to have things that other people want?**
- **What's it like to want other people's things?**
- **How does God want us to treat our things?**
- **When should we give to others? to God?**

Say: **God gives us many things such as clothes, food, houses to** live in, toys, and much more. There's nothing wrong with having nice things. But God warns us not to be greedy with our possessions. God wants us to share with each other and to share with God. Let's enjoy giving right now.

Have the children share the candy bars so that each child has one. Share any extras with another class.

~~~~~~~~~~~~~~~

EXCUSES, EXCUSES

Theme: Excuses

Scripture: Luke 14:16-24

Description: Say: **Let's play a game about excuses. Think about all the excuses people come up with.**

Have the children scatter around the room and toss a lightweight ball back and forth. Whoever catches the ball calls out an excuse that people make, such as "I couldn't turn in my homework because my dog ate it." Then that person tosses the ball to a child who hasn't had the ball yet.

Make sure every child gets a chance to call out an excuse at least once. Play the game for several minutes and encourage the children to be creative and silly with the excuses they think up.

Then retrieve the ball and put it away. Gather the children and sit down. Say: **There's a story in the Bible about excuses. Listen while I read it.** Read the Scripture. Then ask:

● **Why did the people make excuses instead of going to the party?**

Say: **Let's say that the person who gave the party was Jesus and that Jesus was asking people to come and be a part of his kingdom.**

Ask:

● **How do you think Jesus feels when people make excuses about following him and becoming part of his kingdom?**

● **What excuses do people make to keep from following Jesus?**

Say: **Everyone makes excuses to keep from doing things they don't really want to do. But excuses can hurt other people's feelings, and they can hurt us, too. If we keep making excuses instead of doing homework, then we'll never learn the important things we need to know. If we make excuses to Jesus, then we miss out on having a forever relationship with God.**

JOIN UP!

Theme: Gifts

Scripture: Ephesians 4:11-13

Description: Have children stand near each other. Have one child begin by naming one thing he or she is good at, such as playing an instrument, helping others, or reading. Have a second child name what he or she is good at and link arms with the first child. Continue the activity until all the children are connected together. Then say: **Let's see what the Bible says about what joins us together.** Read the Scripture aloud. Ask:

- **How will we be joined together?**
- **What is it like to be joined together in one strong group?**
- **How can God use our special gifts to join us together?**
- **How can we use our gifts to help each other?**

Say: **Each one of you has a special gift and a special place in God's kingdom. When you use your gift, you become a strong link in the structure of the kingdom. When you use your gift, you help to make others strong, too. God has given you a role that no one else has. Let's do our best to be strong links in the kingdom of God.**

YOU BE THE JUDGE

Theme: Judging

Scripture: Romans 14:1-4, 10-12

Description: Have children point to a child wearing whatever you designate. For example, you may designate something red, tennis shoes, something with a zipper, or something with pockets. Be sure not to pick personal characteristics such as blue-eyed children, tall children, short children, or those with curly hair. Keep this activity fast-paced so no one is pointed at for very long.

Say: **Let's find out what God's Word says about pointing out those who are different from us.** Read the passage. Ask:

- **How did you feel when someone pointed at you?**
- **How do you feel if children at school point at you?**
- **Have you ever seen people point at others who walked funny, were uncoordinated, or didn't do well in school?**
- **How do you think those people felt?**
- **How do you think God feels when people point fingers at others and judge them?**
- **What can you do if you see someone who is being pointed at?**

● **What can we do instead of pointing and judging people who are different from us?**

Say: **It's easy to point and laugh at people who are different from us. Some people dress differently, talk differently, and act differently than we do—and sometimes those people stick out because they're different. But God wants us to love and accept all people. Instead of pointing, we can be kind and loving to people who are different from us. And we can stick up for them when others are being unkind.**

NOT TRUE

Theme: Lying

Scripture: John 18:15-18, 25-27

Description: Have children stand in a circle and play a game called Cock-a-Doodle-Doo!

Have one child stand in the middle of the circle and say something that's either true or false about himself or herself, such as "My favorite meal is tacos" or "I like math."

Tell all the other children to clap if they think the statement is true or say "cock-a-doodle-doo!" if they think the statement is false. Then the child who said the statement will tell whether it's true.

Then choose another child to stand in the middle and say something that's either true or false. Play until each child has had a turn in the middle.

Then have the children sit down. Ask:

● **Why do people lie?**

● **How do you know when someone is lying and when someone is telling the truth?**

● **Is it ever OK to tell a lie?**

Say: **Let's see what the Bible says about truth and lies.** Read the Scripture. Then ask:

● **Why didn't Peter tell the truth?**

● **What does God think about lying?**

● **Why does it sometimes take courage to tell the truth?**

Say: **Everyone is tempted to tell a lie sometimes. Many times we feel that if we tell lies we can get out of trouble. But lies only get us into deeper trouble because we have to keep telling them, just as Peter had to lie three times. God will forgive us if we lie, as God forgave Peter. But God is pleased when we tell the truth, and God will help us have enough courage to tell the truth every day.**

CHAPTER 4

OBJECT LESSONS

LOVE GOES AROUND

Theme: Love

Scripture: 1 John 4:7-12

Object: A red construction paper heart for you and each child

Description: Stack all of the hearts and hold them together so it looks like you have only one heart.

Have the children stand in a circle, then you stand in the middle of the circle. Say: **Let's talk about God's love. While I read a passage from the Bible, walk to the right until you hear the word "love." Then stop.**

Read the Scripture aloud and have the children walk to the right. When you read the word "love," "loves," or "loved," have the children stop. Give one of the hearts to a child. Then continue reading the Scripture. Have the children stop each time you read the word "love." Give away one heart each time the children stop. Continue until everyone has a heart (including yourself). If you have more than 13 children in your worship service, give away more than one heart each time the children stop walking. (The word "love" is mentioned 13 times in this Scripture.)

When you have finished reading the passage, have the children sit down. Ask:
- **Who should we love?**
- **What can we do to show love?**
- **What does "God is love" mean?**

Say: **We love each other because God loves us. God is the perfect example of love. When we love others we're showing that God's love is inside of us and that we're God's children. And the more love we give away, the more love we have to give.**

SENSITIVITY PLUS

Theme: Sensitivity

Scripture: 1 Corinthians 8:8-13

Object: One piece of candy; a piece of pizza with meat; and, for each child, a carrot

Description: Show children a piece of candy. Ask:
- **Who can eat candy?**
- **Who isn't allowed to eat a lot of candy?**

Say: **It's not good for anyone to eat a lot of candy. But some people can't eat candy at all because it will make them sick.**

Then show children a piece of pizza. Ask:
- **Who eats pizza?**
- **Can you think of anyone who might not be able to eat pizza?**

Say: **Most people enjoy pizza. But some people can't eat it because they are allergic to an ingredient such as cheese, mushrooms, or tomatoes. Or some people eat a special diet because of their religious beliefs; for example, some Jewish people don't eat anything that has both meat and cheese on it.**

Ask:
- **Have you ever been with someone who was eating something that you weren't allowed to eat?**
- **How did that make you feel?**

Say: **There was a time in the Bible when people were getting very upset over what others ate. Some felt it was evil to eat meat that had been offered to false gods. Other people felt that since the false gods weren't real it didn't matter if they ate the meat. The people got into a big argument. Listen to what the Bible says about the situation.**

Read the Scripture. Ask:
- **How can you be sensitive to people who can't eat or do the same things that you do?**

Ask:
- **Is everyone here allowed to eat carrots?**

Give everyone a carrot to munch on. Say: **We can be sensitive to people who can't do all the things we can do. When we care about others, we try not to tempt them with foods they can't eat, and we try not to make them feel bad. Let's work hard to be kind and sensitive to those around us.**

OLD AND NEW

Theme: Transformation

Scripture: 2 Corinthians 5:17

Object: Paper clips

Description: Hold up a paper clip. Have the children brainstorm all the different uses for a paper clip. Then demonstrate different uses. For example, you might use the paper clip in one girl's hair as a barrette, you could use a paper clip as a bookmark, or you could unbend it and create a Christmas-ornament hanger.

Give the children paper clips and have them make bracelets. Say: **Listen to what the Bible says about new things coming from old things.** Read the Scripture aloud. Ask:

● **What does it mean when it says we become new creations?**
● **Will we look different?**
● **Will we think differently?**
● **Will we act different?**
● **How can something old become new?**
● **How did the paper clips become new?**

Say: **When we become new creations, God makes our insides clean and new. Then we can serve God in ways that we didn't before. Just as the paper clips can be used for things other than just holding papers together, we can do other, more important things when we become new creations in God.**

LAZY DAYS

Theme: Laziness

Scripture: 2 Thessalonians 3:6-13

Object: Grapes, oranges, and a napkin for each child

Description: Form groups of four. Have one child in each group be the "feeder." The other three children are the "eaters." Tell the eaters to act as lazy as possible. Tell the feeders to feed grapes to all of the eaters for one or two minutes. Then ask:

● **Why is it easier to be lazy than to work hard?**
● **How does it feel to help others while they're being lazy?**
● **What's it like to be fed without having to help out?**

Say: **Listen to what the Bible says about being lazy.** Read the Scripture aloud. Ask:

● **Why should we stay away from lazy people?**

● **Why does the Bible say not to get tired of doing good things?**

Bring out several oranges. Have children work together to peel the oranges and separate them into sections. Set the sections on napkins for each child to enjoy.

Say: **God is pleased when we all work hard to help each other. Working together can be fun, too. Now let's enjoy the oranges together.**

EVEN FOR YOU

Theme: Sin

Scripture: Romans 5:6-11

Object: Self-stick notes, pencils, and a cross made out of tagboard

Description: Hang up the cross. Then say: **Listen while I read about Jesus dying for us.** Read the Scripture aloud.

Give each child a self-stick note and a pencil. Have the children write their names on the notes. Then have them think of something wrong that they've done. Have them write an X on the self-stick note to represent the sin. Be ready to help young children who can't write well.

Have children gather around the cross then stick their self-stick notes on the cross. Then go to the cross yourself and read aloud the name on each self-stick note, saying, **Jesus died for** (child's name).

After you've read all the notes, say: **Look at the X's we've put on the cross. When Jesus died on the cross, he took all of our sins with him. He died for us so we wouldn't have to pay the punishment for our sins. Because Jesus died, we can live.**

Have the children join hands while you pray: **Thank you, Jesus, for taking our sins to the cross with you. Thank you for dying for us so we can be God's friends. Amen.**

TOGETHER, TOGETHER

Theme: Unity

Scripture: Galatians 3:26-28

Object: Plastic knives, forks, and spoons—one utensil for each child

Description: Give each child an eating utensil.

Have the "forks" get together in a group and talk about their favorite hobbies. Have the "spoons" get together and talk about their favorite games. Have the "knives" get together and talk about their favorite television shows.

Then have the children break into table-setting groups with a knife, fork, and spoon together in a trio. Have the "table settings" tell one another who lives with them.

Next have children from trios in which two of the utensils are the same and the third is different—two forks and a spoon or two knives and a fork, for example. Have these trios talk about what they like and dislike about school.

Have the children form table-setting groups again and discuss what they like about church.

Then have the children form one big group and sit down. Ask:

● **How are you all different?**

● **How are you all the same?**

Say: **Listen to what the Bible says about being like others.** Read the Scripture. Ask:

● **What does it mean when it says there is no difference between us?**

Say: **Listen while I say the Scripture a different way. Raise your hand when I call out your part.**

You are all God's children because you have faith in Jesus. There is no difference between knife and fork, fork and spoon, or spoon and knife. You are all the same in Jesus.

Have the children all squeeze together in a group hug.

● ● ● ● ● ● ● ● ● ●

HELPING HANDS

Theme: Service

Scripture: Galatians 6:10

Object: Have children bring their mittens on a cold winter day. You'll also need two clothespins for each child and an undecorated Christmas tree or a bare branch from a tree.

Description: Have children form a circle around the tree while holding their mittens. Read the Scripture aloud.

Give each child two clothespins. Say: **Think of a way you can help someone and tell us your idea while you hang a mitten on the tree. Since you have two mittens and two clothespins, you can think of two ideas.**

A child might say, "listening to a friend who is sad," "feeding the hungry," or "cleaning my room." After a child names something and hangs up a mitten, have the group say, "Praise God for helping hands." After all the children have hung up their mittens, read the Scripture aloud again. Ask:

● **Why is it good to help others?**

● **Why is it especially good to help people who follow God?**

● **How does it feel to help someone?**

● **How do you feel when someone helps you?**

● **Why is God happy when we help others?**

Say: **There are many things that we can do every day to help others. We can keep our eyes open so we can see opportunities to help. And we can keep our hands ready.**

WHAT'S IN THERE?

Theme: Believing

Scripture: Hebrews 11:1

Object: A goldfish in a sealed plastic bag filled with water and placed inside a paper bag. You'll also need a coat. If you can't get a goldfish, bring something else the children will have a hard time believing you have inside your coat. For example, you might tape Life Savers candy to your shirt and tell the children that you're wearing a candy shirt.

Description: Wear a coat. Hold the paper bag with the goldfish inside the coat. Tell the children you're keeping a goldfish warm inside your coat. Ask:

● **Do you believe me?**

Then pull out the bag, show the children the goldfish, and ask if they believe you now. Ask:

● **How do you decide when something is true if you can't see it?**

Say: **Listen to what the Bible says about believing things we can't see.** Read the Scripture aloud. Ask:

● **What are some things that you believe in even though you can't see them?**

● **Why does it take faith to believe in Jesus?**

Say: **It takes faith to believe many things. It took faith for you to believe I had a goldfish in my coat. It also takes faith to believe the sun will come up every morning. And we can't see heaven, but God tells us there is a heaven, so we believe it. Listen to what Jesus said about people who believe in him even though they've never seen him.**

Read John 20:29. Ask:

● **What do you think it means when it says we will be happy?**

Say: **When we believe in Jesus and follow him even though we have never seen Jesus, then we have great faith. We'll be happy, too, because Jesus is real and he's worth believing in.**

BEAUTIFUL CHILDREN

Theme: Creation

Scripture: Psalm 139:13-18

Object: Polaroid camera with enough film to photograph each child

Description: Have children stand in a circle and clap to the beat while they say, "God made me. God made you." When children say "me," they should point to themselves. Each time they say "you," they should point to a different child in the circle.

After children have done this for a minute or two, say: **I'm going to take a picture of each one of you. Be sure to smile your biggest smile to praise God.** Take the pictures and put them aside to develop.

Say: **Listen to what the Bible says about how God made us.** Read the Scripture aloud. Pass around the pictures. As children are looking at them, ask:

● **What do you see in the pictures that you like about God's creation?**

● **How does it make you feel to know that God knew you even before you were born?**

● **What do you think is neat about people compared to other things God made?**

● **How can we praise God for making us?**

Choose one child's suggestion for praising God. If the children don't mention anything that can easily be done in a classroom, sing these words to the tune of "This Is the Day."

I am the one, I am the one,
That the Lord has made, that the Lord has made.
I will rejoice, I will rejoice,
And be glad I'm me, and be glad I'm me.
I am the one that the Lord has made.
I will rejoice and be glad I'm me.
I am the one, I am the one,
That the Lord has made.

Say: **God has made us special. Let's hang your pictures on the wall to remind us of God's beautiful creation.**

Hang the pictures at children's eye level.

THE GIFT OF GRACE

Theme: Grace

Scripture: Ephesians 2:8-9

Object: A cereal box with cereal and a surprise (such as a sticker, candy, or toy) inside. You'll also need a cassette player, a cassette tape of lively music, and a surprise like the one in the cereal box for each child.

Description: Have children form a circle. Give one child the cereal box to toss. Have children take turns tossing the cereal box to each other while the music plays. Explain that when you stop the music, the child who has the box will get a surprise.

Play the music for a few minutes while the children toss the box back and forth. Then stop the music. Have the child who's holding the box pull out the surprise. (You may want to provide a bowl for the child in case he or she needs to pour out the cereal to get to the prize.) Pass around the prize and let all of the children look at it. Then ask:

● **What did** (child's name) **do to deserve the prize?**

● **Have you ever gotten a present that was a complete surprise or one that you didn't really deserve?**

● **How does getting presents or winning prizes make you feel?**

Say: **Listen to what the Bible says about a present we've received from God.** Read aloud the Scripture. Ask:

● **What gift has God given to us?**

● **Why don't we deserve it?**

● **Why did God give us such a good gift if we didn't deserve it?**

Give each child a surprise similar to the one in the cereal box.

Say: **God loves us so much that God offers us the gift of eternal life even though we don't deserve it. Let's thank God for the gift.**

Have the children give God a round of applause.

JESUS' STRENGTH

Theme: Helping

Scripture: Philippians 4:13

Object: A glove

Description: Have the children sit on the floor. Put a glove on the floor in front of them. Ask:

● **What can a glove do by itself?**

● **What does a glove need in order to do anything?**

Have the children take turns putting on the glove and showing what the glove can do when a hand is inside it.

Say: **A glove can't do much unless a hand is inside it to give it strength. Listen to what the Bible says about the strength we receive from Jesus.** Read the Scripture. Ask:

● **Who gives us strength?**

● **What can we do with Jesus' strength?**

Say: **Jesus gives us the strength we need to do tough things. Without Jesus' help, we'd be like a glove without a hand inside. But with Jesus' help, we can do anything.**

SPARKLING SMILES

Theme: Happiness

Scripture: Proverbs 17:22

Object: A mirror

Description: Hold up a mirror. Have children take turns smiling into the mirror. Then have children hop around the room. When you yell "two-some smiles," children should each run to the person nearest to them and flash a smile before hopping around the room again. When you yell "three-some smiles," children should find two other children and smile at each other at the same time. Continue the activity for several minutes. Make sure that everyone is smiled at.

Bring children back together and form a circle. Say: **Listen to what the Bible says about being cheerful.** Read the Scripture aloud. Ask:
- **How do you feel when you smile?**
- **How do you feel when others smile?**
- **How can cheerfulness be like good medicine?**

Say: **When people smile at us, we want to smile back. When we smile at others, our hearts feel glad. Being cheerful and having smiles on our faces can make us feel good even when things are going wrong.**

EXTRAORDINARY FUN

Theme: Being content

Scripture: Philippians 4:11-12

Object: A ball of yarn for every four children

Description: Form groups of four and give each group a ball of yarn. Say: **Pretend that this ball of yarn is the only toy you own. Think up games that you can play with the yarn.**

Have each group think of a game and play it. Then have children sit in one big group. Put away the balls of yarn. Have each group describe its game. Some children may have played Catch with it. Others may have designed a maze or unraveled the yarn to see how far it would go. When all the groups have shared, ask:
- **What would you think if this yarn really were your only toy?**
- **What are your favorite toys?**
- **What's your most important possession?**
- **How do you feel when you see others who have lots more than you do?**
- **How do you feel when you see others who don't have as**

much as you do?

Say: **Listen to what the Bible says about how much stuff we have.** Read the Scripture. Then ask:

● **What does it mean to be content?**
● **Is it easy or hard to be content with what we have?**
● **What can you do to feel more content?**

Say: **It's important to be thankful for what we have whether we have a lot or a little. God wants us to be content instead of being whiny and wanting something that someone else has. God knows that when we're dissatisfied with what we have, we have a hard time praising God and serving God. No matter what, we can be content with the things we have.**

OUR FRIEND, THE GUINEA PIG

Theme: Caring

Scripture: Proverbs 12:10a

Object: A guinea pig or other small animal in a cage. You'll also need food, tissues, and anything else used to care for the animal.

Description: Ask children to explain how animals should be treated. Say: **Listen to what the Bible says about taking care of animals.** Read the Scripture aloud. Ask:

● **What do we need to do to care for this pet?**

Have the group meet the pet's needs. They can feed the animal, pet it, talk to it, or leave it alone. They can also shred tissues for a bed for the animal. Afterward, ask:

● **How often do you take care of animals?**
● **How do you take care of animals if you don't have a pet?**
● **Why does God say it's good to take care of animals?**

Say: **Animals are as much a part of God's creation as we are. It's important for us to care for our pets—to make sure they have enough food and water and to make sure their homes are warm and comfortable. God is pleased when we take care of God's creation.**

CHAPTER 5

MUSIC IDEAS

SINGING VOLUMES

As you sing any song, have children stand tall with their arms extended above their heads. Have children sing as loudly as they can. Then have children gradually sing more softly as they let their arms slowly fall to the floor and then bend over. Have children whisper the song as they bend low near the floor. Then have children gradually raise their arms and increase the volume. Try moving up and down quickly while singing the song. End by singing the song through slowly.

TOUCH AND LOVE

Sing "Jesus Loves Me." The second time through, have children clap twice instead of singing the word "Jesus." The third time through, have children fold their arms across their chest instead of singing the word "me." The fourth time through, have children hug a friend instead of singing the word "loves." (Be sure that everyone has a friend to hug!) The fifth time through, have children do all three actions as they sing.

MUSICAL WALTZ

Choose a familiar song such as "God Is So Good" or "This Is the Day." (Both of these songs are in *The Group Songbook,* available from Group Publishing, Inc.) Ask one-third of your children to be the tubas. Have them sing "oom-pah-pah, oom-pah-pah" in a waltz beat. Have them sing low like tubas. Have another third of your children be flutes. Have them sing "do-do-do, do-do-do" smoothly and at a higher pitch. Have the other third of your children sing the words to the song. Lead children in singing the song with the oom-pah-pahs and the do-do-dos. You might want to have an adult lead each section. It takes a bit of coordination to get all three parts going. The results are fun even if they aren't perfect.

NEW WORDS

Sing the familiar song "Down in My Heart." The first time through, have children jump each time they sing the word "joy." For the second verse, have children sing, "I have a smile, smile, smile, smile right on my face (where?)" while smiling at a different person each time they sing the word "smile." For the third verse, have children sing, "I have to praise, praise, praise, praise God every day (when?)" while lifting and shaking their hands in the air each time they sing the word "praise." For the fourth verse, have children sing, "I have a hug, hug, hug, hug to give to you (who?)" while hugging a different person each time they sing the word "hug."

MAKE AND PLAY

Have children make instruments out of construction toys or other classroom toys or supplies. If children need creative ideas, suggest that they make tambourines, drums, shakers, and rattles. Then have children play their instruments while singing their favorite songs.

EVERYWHERE PRAISE

Sing these words to the familiar tune of "Praise Him, Praise Him":

Praise God, Praise God,
Praise God when we're crying,
Praise God when we're happy.
Praise God, Praise God,
Praise God when we're happy or we're sad.

Praise God, Praise God,
Praise God when we're at church,
Praise God when we're at home.
Praise God, Praise God,
Praise God when we're at school or at play.

Praise God, Praise God,
Praise God 'cause we love you,
Praise God 'cause we need you.
Praise God, Praise God,
We praise you 'cause you're such a great God.

KITCHEN BAND

Take children to your church kitchen. Encourage them to choose various pots, pans, lids, and utensils to use as instruments to praise God. (Monitor the volume, however.) Have the children use the creative instruments as they sing.

A SHAKIN' BALLOON

Put a small handful of uncooked rice in a deflated balloon (a kitchen funnel makes this easy to do). Then inflate the balloon. Have children stand in a circle, bat the balloon, and sing a song. The rice inside the balloon will add the accompaniment.

WEATHER MUSIC

Praise and worship God by imitating natural elements. Have children make the sounds of natural elements by doing the activities in parentheses: a light rain (softly slap legs), a thunderstorm (shout booming sounds), a blizzard (make swishing sounds and twirl around the room), a tornado (spin and whoosh), a warm sunny day (stand still, smile, and hold arms over heads like the sun), a breeze (gently blow and jog around the room), and a heavy rain (slap legs loudly and hard).

Afterward, have children shout, "God, thank you for weather!"

ANIMAL SING-A-LONG

Have children sing a well-known song using only the sounds of one particular animal instead of the words. For example, "meow, meow," "woof, woof," "hoot, hoot," or "tweet, tweet." Sing the song several times, using a different animal sound each time.

AFFIRMATION SONG

Have children stand in two lines facing each other about two feet apart. Sing the classic children's song "He's Got the Whole World" substituting the name of a child for the words "the whole world." For example, sing, "He's got our Joanie in his hands. He's got our Joanie in his hands." While the children sing, the child who is named walks between the two rows. The children on both sides reach out their hands and gently pat the child's back as the child passes by. Encourage children not to be rough as they pat. Repeat the song until every child has been sung about.

NEAR AND FAR

Have children form trios. Choose a song to sing three times. The first time, have children in each group whisper the song in each other's ears. The second time, have children hold hands while skipping in a circle. The third time, have children separate as far as they can and sing the song loudly.

INSTRUMENT MEDLEY

Have each child choose a musical instrument to imitate. Then choose a well-known song and, instead of singing the words, have children pretend they're playing their instruments. Encourage each child to imitate the instrument's pitch, type of music, and volume while acting out how the instrument is played. Then have certain instruments join together as duets, trios, quartets, and full orchestras as you "sing" the song several times. You can also have a few children sing the words as the instruments accompany them.

PERCUSSION MOUTHS

Have children hum a favorite song with their mouths open in an O shape. Have them tap their hands over their mouths, flick the inside of their cheeks, or snap their fingers against the outside of their cheeks in time to their humming. Have children experiment to see how the sounds change when they tap faster and slower on their cheeks. Others could blow across the tops of bottles to keep the rhythm.

HOPPIN' HALLELU

Sing the song "Hallelu, Hallelu" with your children. (The words and chords appear in *Ready, Set…Sing!* edited by Mary M. Nicol and Pamela K. Roth, published by Judson Press, Valley Forge, PA.) Form two groups. Have one group sing the word "Hallelu." Have the second group sing, "Praise Ye the Lord." The second time through, have children use kazoos instead of singing. Simple kazoos can be made by wrapping wax paper around the end of toilet paper tubes and attaching it with rubber bands. The third time through, have the children clap and stomp the rhythm of "Hallelu" and "Praise Ye the Lord."

DRUMMER'S DELIGHT

Have children stand in a circle facing the back of the person in front of them as they sing. Have children keep the beat of the song by tapping the person's back like a drum. Make sure children don't get too rough. The vibration will probably make children giggle.

12 DAYS OF WORSHIP

Have the children think of 12 ways they worship God on Sunday. Write the ideas on newsprint. For example, kids might say, "We pray silently" or "We sing happy songs." Then sing a variation of "The Twelve Days of Christmas" using these words:

On the first hour of Sunday,
We worshiped God like this . . .

Sing through the entire list of items in the style of "The Twelve Days of Christmas."

STACCATO SMOOTHIE

Choose a favorite song and have children sing it in different ways. Try short, choppy sounds; smooth sounds that all run together; a quick tempo; a slow tempo; a monotone so all the notes have the same pitch; or with a lot of expression, like an opera singer. You could even sing the song in a free-for-all in which children sing together, but they each sing the song in whatever melody and tempo they want.

WHAT A DAY!

Sing the following words to the tune of "This Is the Day." Have the children clap, stomp, and shake hands as indicated by the lyrics.

This is the day, this is the day
That you really made great, that you really made great.
Now we all clap, now we all clap
And are glad in it, and are glad in it.
This is the day that you really made great.
Now we all clap and are glad in it.
This is the day, this is the day
That you really made great.

This is the day, this is the day
That you really made great, that you really made great.
Now we all stomp, now we all stomp
And are glad in it, and are glad in it.
This is the day that you really made great.
Now we all stomp and are glad in it.
This is the day, this is the day
That you really made great.

This is the day, this is the day
That you really made great, that you really made great.
Now we shake hands, now we shake hands
And are glad in it, and are glad in it.
This is the day that you really made great.
Now we shake hands and are glad in it.
This is the day, this is the day
That you really made great.

CHAPTER 6

CREATIVE MOVEMENT IDEAS

RAINBOW WEAVERS

Theme: The Body of Christ joined together

Cut a 5-foot piece of crepe paper for each child. Use several different colors of paper. Fasten one end of each crepe paper strip securely to the top of a yardstick, stick, or pole.

Have one child hold the pole overhead while the other children each pick up one end of a piece of crepe paper. Have the children holding the crepe paper back away from the pole and hold their crepe paper high in the air so that the strips are almost parallel to the floor.

Number the children as ones or twos. Have the ones take one step forward, walk past the neighbor on the left, and then take one step backward to rejoin the twos in the circle.

Then have the twos take one step forward, walk past the neighbor on the right, and then take one step backward to rejoin the ones in the circle.

Have the children continue to alternate these movements to wrap the crepe paper strips around the pole. As the crepe paper strips are woven around the pole, they'll get shorter. Have the children move closer to the pole until the crepe paper strips are completely wrapped around it.

You'll have a beautiful weaving of color down the pole when the children have finished. Tape the ends to the bottom of the pole and keep the weaving in your worship area to remind the children of how the body of Christ is woven together.

MIRROR IMITATION

Theme: Praise

Form pairs. Have one partner do actions to praise God while the other partner imitates the movements. Children might clap their hands or say "I love you" to God in sign language. Play praise music in the background. Then have partners trade roles and repeat the process.

PAINT AND SCULPT

Theme: Appearances

Form pairs. Have one partner slump over, emotionless and motionless. Have the other partner move the child's body to "sculpt" the child into a Christian. If children are stumped, ask:
- **What kinds of facial expressions do Christians have?**
- **How does a Christian stand?**
- **What would the arms look like? the legs?**

Children will come to realize that Christians aren't outwardly different from other people. This is a good jumping-off point for a discussion about the inner qualities that make Christians truly different.

JOYFUL COLORS

Theme: Joy

Have the children brainstorm reasons to be joyful. Then give each child a scarf or a strip of crepe paper. Have children stand in a line. The child standing at the front of the line leads the others in doing joyful movements with the scarf as you play lively, joyful music. (Play music that varies in loudness and tempo.) The leader might move quickly and hold the scarf high, stop and shake the scarf, wave the scarf up and down, or hold the scarf at both ends and wave it back and forth.

LANGUISH LAMENT

Theme: Repentance

Form groups of four. Say: **Bow your heads, hold hands, and slowly walk around in a circle. Think about something that you're sorry you did.** Pause while children do the actions. **Now drop to your knees and let go of each other's hands.** Pause. **Hunch down into a tiny ball. Think of how God feels when we do wrong.** Pause. **Hold**

a fist out to the middle of the circle. Pause. **Now open your fist and slowly uncurl your body so that you're kneeling again. Silently tell God you're sorry.** Pause. **Together, build a tower with all of your hands and think of God's forgiveness.** Pause.

STUFFED ANIMAL ROMP

Theme: Giving comfort

Ask children to bring their favorite stuffed animals to your worship time. Find out if you can use several stuffed animals from the nursery if you need a few extra.

Have children stand in a large circle with about two feet between them and place their stuffed animals on the floor in front of them.

Say: **Sometimes we feel sad. Think about what it's like to feel sad.** Pause. **Sometimes we feel all alone—like no one cares. Think about what it's like to feel alone.** Pause.

Now hug your stuffed animal and think about what makes you feel better when you're sad and alone. Pause.

We can also help others when they feel sad and alone. Find a partner and give him or her your stuffed animal. Think about how it feels to help others. Pause. Then have partners exchange stuffed animals.

God is pleased when we comfort others when they feel sad and alone.

RIBBON ZAG

Theme: Thankfulness

For every 10 children, use a piece of ribbon at least 12 feet long. Have the children hold the ribbon at waist level with one hand.

Say: **Let's show how thankful we are for God's gifts.**

● **Move to the left to show you're thankful for the sun.**

● **Move to the right to show you're thankful for clouds.**

● **Hold the ribbon above your head to show you're thankful for winter.**

● **Now hold the ribbon down low to show you're thankful for summer.**

● **Hold the ribbon waist high to show you're thankful for spring.**

● **Hold it neck high to show you're thankful for fall.**

● **Wiggle the ribbon to show you're thankful for rain.**

● **Now hold the ribbon still to show you're thankful for snow.**

● **Make a circle and hold the ribbon high as you say with me, "God, we're thankful for all the things you bring us. Amen."**

MiNE TO YOURS

Theme: Giving

Practice this motion with children. Have children curl their hands in toward their chests and then slowly stretch out their arms and extend their hands as if they are giving something away.

Have children do this motion by themselves. Then have them pair up and do the motion toward each other. Next have pairs form foursomes and have each member of the foursome do the motion toward the middle of the group.

Continue having the groups match up with other groups until the entire class is in one circle doing the motion. While the children are in the circle, read Deuteronomy 15:7-8 aloud.

End with the group squeezing close together so children's outstretched hands are together in the middle of the circle.

GOD'S AMAZING WORLD

Theme: Praise

Give each child one sheet of construction paper. Use only yellow, blue, brown, and green construction paper. Have children stand in a line, side by side.

Tell children to take one step forward and hold the paper above their heads when its color corresponds to an item in the reading. When a different color is mentioned, they are to step back.

Say: **We praise you, God, for the sun above** (pause), **the grass below** (pause), **the soil** (pause) **for food to grow, and water** (pause) **to drink. You've made wonderful animals such as canaries** (pause), **frogs** (pause), **blue jays** (pause), **and bears** (pause). **You've made chocolate** (pause), **blueberries** (pause), **lettuce** (pause), **and bananas** (pause). **For all these amazing things, we praise you. Thank you for making our world such a colorful one.**

COTTON BALL SQUASH

Theme: Forgiveness

Give each child two cotton balls. Have children do the actions in parentheses as you read these statements:

● **Sometimes we're careless and we mess up.** (Toss one cotton ball onto the floor.)

● **Please forgive us, God.** (Rub the other cotton ball on a cheek.)

● **Sometimes we step on other people's treasures.** (Step on other children's cotton balls on the floor.)

● **Please forgive us, God.** (Rub a cotton ball on a cheek.)

● **Sometimes we take things that aren't ours.** (Take another child's cotton ball.)

● **Please forgive us, God.** (Rub a cotton ball on a cheek.)

● **Sometimes we throw things when we get mad.** (Throw the cotton balls on the floor.)

● **Please forgive us, God.** (Rub a cotton ball on a cheek.)

● **Sometimes we keep our things for ourselves instead of sharing them.** (Hide the cotton balls.)

● **Please forgive us, God.** (Rub a cotton ball on a cheek.)

● **For all these things, please forgive us, God.** (Rub a cotton ball on a cheek.)

PUZZLED NO MORE

Theme: Cooperation

Mark one of these colors on the back of each piece of an easy puzzle: blue, green, yellow, red, brown, purple, and orange.

Give each child a puzzle piece. Make sure you distribute all the puzzle pieces. It's OK if children have more than one puzzle piece, but all their puzzle pieces should be the same color.

Have the children act out this story according to the colors on their puzzle pieces.

Say: **The yellow pieces wanted to put the puzzle together. The yellow pieces jumped once, marched in place for three steps, and then skipped to place their pieces on the table.** (Pause.) **The green pieces flapped their arms while skipping around the room. Then the green pieces joined the yellow pieces, trying to make a good fit of their puzzle pieces.** (Pause.) **Meanwhile, the blue pieces just started walking.** (Pause.)

The red pieces sang four notes before joining the yellows and greens (pause), **and the brown pieces walked behind the blue pieces for a while before joining into the puzzle fun.** (Pause.) **The purple pieces twirled around twice before joining the puzzle** (pause), **and the orange pieces rolled on the floor to get to the puzzle.** (Pause.)

And since those blue pieces were still walking around (pause), **the other pieces joined together and said, "Blues, please stop and cooperate!"** (Pause.) **And so they did. And all the pieces finally came together to make one puzzle.** (Pause.)

Have children work to put the puzzle together.

FEATHERS AWAY

Theme: Joyful praise

Give each child a feather. Play lively music and have the children wave their feathers, twirl them, and blow on them to keep them in the air. Then have the children all toss their feathers at the same time. As the feathers float down to the ground, have the children think of how God sends good things to them.

PINWHEEL PRAISE

Theme: Praise

Tie a 1-foot crepe paper streamer to each wrist of each child, then have children stand in a circle. Play upbeat worship music that the children know. Have children make circles with their right hands, moving to the music, then do the same with their left hands. Then have them move both hands at the same time. Then have children turn around while waving both arms.

Have children make a large pinwheel by holding left hands in the middle of the circle. As they walk around in a circle, have the children wave their right arms. Reverse the pinwheel by walking backward. Then have children turn around, hold right hands, and wave their left hands. Once they are comfortable with the motions, have the children sing the song as they walk and wave.

CHAPTER 7

HOLIDAY IDEAS

RIVERS OF JUSTICE AND GOODNESS

Theme: Justice

Holiday: Martin Luther King Jr. Day

Scripture: Amos 5:24

Description: Have children sit in a circle. Say: **When we celebrate Martin Luther King Jr. Day, we remember a person who worked hard to bring justice to the world. That means he tried very hard to help people who were treated unfairly. Let's hear what the Bible has to say about fairness and justice.** Read Amos 5:24. Ask:

- **What does it mean when it says that fairness should be like a river?**

Say: **Let's talk about things that are unfair, then we'll wash away the unfairness in our own "river of justice."**

Have children take turns naming something that hurts children, such as name-calling, hitting, or teasing. After something is named, have the children "wash it away" by wiggling their fingers in front of them from right to left, again and again. After many injustices have been washed away, read the verse again. Ask:

- **How does it feel to be treated unfairly?**
- **How would it feel to have the injustice washed away?**
- **How is goodness like an ever-flowing stream?**
- **How can we help others who are treated unfairly?**

Say: **Unfairness and injustice exist all over the world. That makes God unhappy. God wants us to be fair and just in everything we do. The Bible says that fairness should be like a river and goodness should be like a stream that never stops. Let's** work as hard as **Martin Luther King Jr.** did to bring goodness that never stops and to wash away injustice in a river of fairness.

WHAT WE LIKE BEST

Theme: Love

Holiday: Valentine's Day

Scripture: John 13:34-35

Description: Form groups of four. Have each group form a heart—one child stands at the bottom to represent the heart's point, two children stand where the humps should be, and the fourth child stands in the middle where the two humps meet. Have the children hold hands throughout this activity. Have group members each say one thing they like about the person standing in the middle, such as "I like the way you laugh" or "You have a great smile." After everyone has said one thing, have all the children move one place to the right so a different child stands in the middle. Repeat the activity until everyone has been affirmed.

Have the children remain in their foursomes and sit down. Say: **Let's see what the Bible says about love.** Read the Scripture aloud. Ask:

● **Why is it good to love each other?**

● **How does our love for each other show that we're Jesus' disciples?**

● **What can you do to show love for each other?**

Say: **We talk a lot about love on Valentine's Day. As Christians, we have more reason to celebrate love than anyone else because the Bible says that God *is* love. When we show love to each other, we're showing that we care about God and that we obey God's command to love one another.**

PRAISE THE KING

Theme: Praise

Holiday: Palm Sunday

Scripture: John 12:12-15

Description: Give each child a palm branch. Stand in a circle with the children and have them wave their palm branches up and down. Then have children turn around and wave their palm branches up and down outside the circle. While they do this, have children say, "Hosanna. Hosanna. Jesus is king."

Then break away from the circle and have the children follow you for a game of Follow the Leader. Tell the children to follow your motions.

Lead the group in moving the palm branches in ways that reflect praise. For example, you might hold the palm branch by its ends and raise it up and down above your head. You might "do the wave" with the palm branch. You might bow with the palm branch stretched out in front of you. You might also skip and make a sweeping motion in front of you with the palm branch.

Re-form the circle and end the activity by waving the palm branches up and down in the middle of the circle. Read the Scripture aloud. Ask:

● **What's it like to praise Jesus with a palm branch?**

● **How would you have felt on the first Palm Sunday if you had been there?**

● **How do you think Jesus felt when everyone praised him with palm branches?**

● **Why did the people praise Jesus?**

● **Why do we praise Jesus?**

● **What are other ways we can praise Jesus?**

Say: **We praise Jesus because he is the king, the Messiah that came to save the world from sin and from death. Jesus is perfect. He never sinned, and he loved us all enough to die for our sins. Those are pretty good reasons to praise him. Let's praise him once more.**

Have the children wave their branches and shout "Hosanna."

A PAINFUL GOODBYE

Theme: Pain

Holiday: Good Friday

Scripture: Matthew 27:27-35, 45-50

Description: You'll need a bowl of ashes for this activity, along with napkins or plastic bags.

Form pairs. Say: **Today we're talking about Good Friday—the day Jesus died. We'll use ashes in this activity because in biblical times, people put ashes on themselves to show they were sad.**

Have one partner from each pair come forward and put a spoonful of ashes on a napkin or in a plastic bag.

Say: **As I read this story aloud, take turns putting ashes on each other as I give you instructions. Do this slowly and gently as you remember how Jesus suffered.**

Say: **On Good Friday, people set a crown of thorns on Jesus' head.** Have partners dip their fingers in the ashes and put an ash mark in the shape of a cross on each other's forehead.

Then they nailed Jesus's hands to a wooden cross. Have partners put ash marks on each other's hands.

Bring children together in a circle. Read the Scripture aloud. Ask:

- **How did you feel when you thought about the holes the nails made in Jesus' hands?**
- **How do you think Jesus felt?**
- **What do you think about when you see the cross on your partner's forehead?**
- **What does Jesus' death on the cross mean to you?**

End by saying: **We hold out our hands and remember how Jesus' hands were pierced with nails. And we look at a friend and see the cross. We remember Good Friday, and we remember the pain that Jesus suffered so that we can live with him forever.**

BUBBLES FOR JOY

Theme: Joy

Holiday: Easter

Scripture: Luke 24:1-10

Description: Give each child a bottle of bubbles along with a wand to make bubbles. Have children stand in a circle. Tell children not to start making bubbles until you tell them to.

Say: **On Easter morning, it was early when the first people came to where the stone was rolled away. When the women saw what had happened, they were excited. Angels told them that Jesus had risen.** Point to two children, indicating that they are to continuously blow bubbles. **They quickly hurried to tell another person about the news.** Point to the child to the left of the two children blowing bubbles, indicating that he or she is to join them in blowing bubbles.

That person then ran to tell another. Point to the next child on the left, indicating that he or she is to join in. **Then the four told a fifth.** Point to the next child on the left. Continue this pattern until the entire circle is blowing bubbles. Then signal everyone to stop for a moment.

Say: **It's Easter. Spread the good news that Jesus has risen and we can all be joyful.** Signal to the entire group to blow bubbles. Then signal the children to stop.

Say: **Listen to how the story is written in the Bible.** Read the Scripture aloud. Ask:

- **How do you like blowing bubbles?**
- **Which was more exciting: when a few people were blowing bubbles or when everyone was blowing bubbles? Explain.**
- **Why is Easter such a joyful time?**
- **Why is the news about Jesus such happy news?**

● **What can we do to be joyful at Easter?**

Say: **The women were surprised to discover that Jesus wasn't in the tomb anymore. And they were joyful when they found out that he had risen from the dead. They spread the news to everyone. We can spread the joyful news, too.**

EASTER JOY

Theme: Praise

Holiday: Easter

Scripture: Luke 24:13-35

Description: Say: **It's Easter! Let's jump for joy.**

Have children stand in a line facing the back of the person in front of them. Have the children number off by twos.

Have the ones jump to the right and call out, "He is risen." Then have the twos jump to the left and call out, "He is risen indeed." Then have all the children jump back to their original places in line.

Have each child think of a reason to rejoice about Easter. Have the first person in line call out his or her reason and then run to the back of the line. Then have the second person mention his or her reason and run to the back of the line. Continue until everyone has called out a reason and has run to the back of the line.

End the activity with the ones jumping to the right and saying, "He is risen" and the twos responding by jumping to the left and calling out, "He is risen indeed."

Repeat the activity once or twice and speed it up a little each time.

Say: **Listen to this Bible story about what happened after Jesus rose from the dead.** Read the Scripture aloud. Ask:

● **What would you have thought if Jesus came and talked to you after he died and rose from the dead?**

● **The disciples didn't know it was Jesus at first. Do you think you would have recognized Jesus? Why or why not?**

● **Why are Christians excited about Jesus' rising from the dead?**

● **What would our faith be like if Jesus hadn't risen from the dead?**

● **What can we do to celebrate Jesus' rising from the dead?**

Say: **Jesus' followers were so confused about all that had happened that they told it all to a man they met. It turned out that the man was Jesus. Imagine how surprised they were. Think of how happy they must have been when they saw that Jesus really was alive again. We can be full of joy, too, because Jesus' resurrection brings us life.**

ReMeMBeR Me

Theme: Death

Holiday: Memorial Day

Scripture: Isaiah 25:6-8

Description: Cut out pictures from your church directory (or a photocopy of it) of members who've died within the past year. Paste the pictures on a piece of cardboard. Have children stand in a circle and place the pictures in the middle of the circle. Give each child a flower.

Prompt children to say together, "We remember these Christians who used to be with us," and to name each person by saying, "Thank you, God, for the life of (person's name)." After each person is mentioned, have a child put a flower near his or her picture. Continue until a flower has been placed near each picture.

Then say: **Thank you, God, for the lives of people we have known and who have died.** Encourage children to name others who have died then place their flowers next to the cardboard with the pictures.

Then read the Scripture aloud. Say: **Let's pretend that all of these people who have died are having a picnic on a mountainside, just as the Bible describes. Think about how God will wipe every tear from every face.** Ask:

- **What do you think these people will do at the picnic?**
- **Are the people happy or sad? Explain.**
- **How do you feel when people die?**
- **What do you do to remember these people?**
- **How can we thank God for these people?**

Say: **We are sad when people we care about die, because we know that we won't see them again while we're living. But we can remember those people and how much fun we had with them when they were here. There's more good news, too, because God takes care of those who follow him. Christians can look forward to life with God in heaven and a time when God will take away all sadness.**

TiMe FOR EveRYTHiNG

Theme: Moms

Holiday: Mother's Day

Scripture: Proverbs 31:14-21, 25-29

Description: Have children stand in a circle and jump up and down while saying, "We love our moms. We love our moms."

Then have everyone crouch down in a squatting position. Have the child on your left jump up and shout out one thing he or she likes about his or her mom, such as "She gives me hugs" or "She's a great cook."

The entire group responds by jumping up and saying, "We love our moms. We love our moms." Then they all quickly crouch down again. The child to the left of the first child jumps up and shouts out something about his or her mom. And the entire group jumps up again and repeats the saying. Continue until all the children have shared something about their moms.

Say: **The Bible talks about all the things that women do. Listen and see if your mom does any of these things.** Read the Scripture aloud. Ask:

● **How is your mom like the woman in the Bible passage? How is she different?**

● **Why do we like our moms?**

● **How do our moms help us?**

● **How can we show our moms how much we appreciate them?**

End by having the children crouch down, jump up, and say, "Thank you, God, for our moms!"

Note: If some children in your class don't have moms, focus this activity on being thankful for female caregivers such as teachers, aunts, stepmoms, grandmothers, older sisters, and neighbors.

▲ ▲ ▲ ▲ ▲ ▲ ▲ ▲

HOORAY FOR DADS

Theme: Dads

Holiday: Father's Day

Scripture: Proverbs 4:1

Description: You will need a necktie for this activity. Have children stand in a circle. Have the child on your right go to the middle of the circle and say one thing he or she likes about his or her dad. The child then throws a necktie into the air, shouts the name of another child, and runs to take that person's spot in the circle. The child named runs to the middle to catch the tie. Then it's the new child's turn to mention something about his or her dad.

Hint: The tie is easier to throw in the air if it is wadded up in a ball.

Continue until each child has had a turn. Say: **Let's see what the Bible says about dads.** Read the Scripture aloud. Ask:

● **Why is it good to listen to our dads?**

● **How do dads help us?**

● **What's good about dads?**

End by having the children say, "Thank you, God, for dads. Amen."

Note: If some children in your class don't have dads, focus this activity on being thankful for male caregivers such as teachers, grandfathers, uncles, stepdads, neighbors, and older brothers.

FReedoM RiNGs

Theme: Freedom

Holiday: Independence Day

Scripture: Exodus 14:21-31

Description: Have children stand in a circle, hold hands, and walk to the right while you read the story that begins in the next paragraph. Tell children that when you say the word "freedom" they are to let go of each other's hands and start twirling around while moving as far from the circle as they can. When they reach the far ends of the room, they are to run back to the circle, hold hands, and walk in the circle again as you continue the story.

Say: **Sometimes we feel like we're going in a circle. Others tell us what to do, and we feel we have no choices. We don't like that. It gets boring. But then, we're given freedom!** Pause while children twirl and then come back to the circle.

A long time ago, the people in America felt trapped. The British were telling them what to do and how to live. They didn't like it at all. So they fought for their freedom! Pause while children twirl and then come back to the circle.

In biblical times, the Israelites were trapped because they were slaves in Egypt. They thought no one would help them, but God sent Moses and helped them escape to freedom! Pause while children twirl and then come back to the circle.

Have the children sit down. Say: **Let's find out how freedom came to the Israelites.** Read the Scripture aloud. Ask:

● **How did the people feel before Moses parted the sea?**

● **What do you think they thought when they crossed the sea and escaped from the Egyptians?**

● **When do you feel trapped?**

● **How does it feel to be set free?**

● **What do we mean when we say we have freedom because we live in America?**

End by having children stand and twirl in a circle when you say the word "free." Say: **On Independence Day, we celebrate living in a country where we are free to say what we think and where we are free to worship God. Thank you, God, for letting us live in a free country. Amen.**

CIRCLES OF THANKS

Theme: Thankfulness

Holiday: Thanksgiving

Scripture: Psalm 95:2-3

Description: Give each child some circle stickers. (Try to get a variety of colors.) Have children skip around the room. When you shout, "It's thanking time," children are to stop and pair up with someone close to them. Have children say one thing they're thankful for about their partners and then place a sticker on their partners' arms. Then have the children begin skipping again.

Call out, "It's thanking time" several times. Have children pair up with a different child each time. Soon the children will have dots all over their arms. Talk about how the stickers show how much we have to be thankful for.

● **How did it feel to place stickers on other children's arms and explain why you're thankful for them?**

● **How did it feel to receive stickers and thanks?**

Say: **Listen to this Bible passage and be ready to tell me what we can do when we're thankful.** Read the Scripture aloud. Ask:

● **What can we do when we're thankful?**

● **If you put a circle on your arm for everything you're thankful for about God, what would your arm look like?**

● **How do you think God feels when we give thanks to God?**

● **Why is it good to give thanks?**

Say: **God has given us many things to be thankful for. Look around and see all the friends in this room. We're thankful for friends, food, clothes, toys, and families. There are so many good things, we can't count them all. Let's remember to thank God during our Thanksgiving holiday.**

PENNY POWER

Theme: Thankfulness

Holiday: Thanksgiving

Scripture: I Thessalonians 5:16-18

Description: Ask each child to bring 10 pennies. Have extras on hand for visitors and for children who forget theirs. Have each child hold one penny. Ask:

● **How heavy is the penny?**

● **How much could you buy with a penny?**

● **If you saw a penny on the floor, would you pick it up? Why or why not?**

Place an offering plate in the middle of the room on the floor. Have children form a circle around the offering plate and walk around it while shaking their pennies in their hands. When you shout out a child's name, have that child run to the offering plate, name something he or she is thankful for, and place all 10 pennies in the offering plate before rejoining the circle. Continue the activity until every child has put his or her pennies in the offering plate.

Then pass around the offering plate for each child to hold. Say: **Listen to what the Bible says about being thankful.** Read the Scripture aloud. Ask:

● **How heavy is this offering plate full of pennies?**
● **How much could you buy with all these pennies?**
● **What do you think God thinks about all these pennies?**
● **What do we have to be thankful for?**

Have the children carry their offering plate full of pennies to the altar during your church's worship service.

COLORFUL REMEMBRANCES

Theme: Gifts

Holiday: Christmas

Scripture: Matthew 2:1-11

Description: Bring an undecorated Christmas tree for your worship area. Give each child a different-colored ball of yarn. Have children stand around the tree and name gifts from God that are the same color as the ball of yarn. For example if the yarn is red, a child might say, "Cherries, red licorice, and sunsets." Keep going until each child has named at least two or three gifts.

Then have the children decorate the tree by unraveling their yarn and draping it on the tree like a garland. Afterward, admire the colorful tree. Name the different colors one at a time. Each time, have children thank God for all the colorful gifts at Christmastime.

Then read the Scripture aloud. Ask:

● **Why did people bring gifts to Jesus?**
● **Why do you give gifts to other people?**
● **Why do people give gifts to you?**
● **What gifts could you give to Jesus?**

Say: **At Christmastime, we celebrate the best gift of all—Jesus. We celebrate God's gift by giving gifts to each other. This year let's remember to thank God for Jesus, and let's also give a gift to Jesus.**

SECTION 2: USING PUPPETS FOR WORSHIP

Eight-year-old Jeremy hadn't spoken in two years—and no one knew why. But his parents kept him in school, church, and other activities—hoping that one day he would break his silence.

His Christian education teacher could tell Jeremy enjoyed coming to class each Sunday. He listened intently, and she could tell that certain Bible stories touched him by the way his eyes lit up.

One Sunday, a puppet troupe led the worship service. Captivated by the Bible stories, the children listened intently. And since the troupe believed in interactive puppetry, the puppets asked the children questions and got them involved. At one point, one of the full-body puppets came into the audience. After speaking to a number of children, the puppet approached Jeremy.

"What's your name?" asked the puppet, who happened to be a monkey.

Jeremy just smiled.

"It's OK," the puppet said. "Sometimes it's scary to talk. Did you know I didn't talk for a long time? But as you can tell, things are different now. My mom says she can never get me to quit talking!"

The other children started to laugh.

The puppet then leaned closer to Jeremy, put his arms around Jeremy, and whispered into his ear, "I think you're pretty special."

"You are, too!" Jeremy blurted out.

Everyone turned, and a hush filled the room. From that moment on, Jeremy spoke. And his teacher contends it never would have happened without that silly monkey puppet.

WHY PUPPETS?

Puppets are a powerful way to minister to children in a worship setting. Vivacious and vibrant puppets can do a number of things that an adult teacher would have a much harder time doing. Puppets can

● **encourage children to relate in more spontaneous, honest ways.** Sometimes children are suspicious and afraid of adults. Because puppets are usually smaller than children, children often think they "take care" of puppets or that puppets are their peers.

● **role play difficult issues more easily.** One teacher struggled to find ways to get the children to stop hitting and poking each other. Lectures didn't work. Bible stories didn't work. But puppets got the message across. After children got to know a number of puppets through worship, they became very upset when their favorite puppet was hit and poked by another puppet. Now when children start to hit or poke, the teacher brings out the favorite puppet, and the roughhousing stops.

● **make Bible stories more exciting.** Puppets bring both the Old and New Testaments to life. It's best, however, to have the puppet play the role of the actual biblical character rather than a contemporary character acting out a Bible story. Mixing time periods is too confusing to children.

● **present Christian issues without being preachy.** Puppets can tackle tough issues such as sexuality, drug and alcohol use, swearing, and stealing without sounding condemning. It's not appropriate, though, for puppets to have faith commitment experiences, take Communion, or pretend to be baptized. Instead, have puppets discuss, ask questions, and encourage children to participate in exploring important Christian issues.

In the following pages, you'll find eight fun, involving puppet skits to enjoy as you lead children in worship.

ARE YOU DYING?

Theme: Worrying

Scripture: "Give all your worries to him, because he cares about you" (1 Peter 5:7).

Synopsis: Camile worries about her mom, who's sick a lot.

Characters:
  Camile—the daughter
  Janese—Camile's best friend
  Camile's Mom

Props: A bouquet of flowers (either real or artificial), a small blanket, and a few small toys

■ ■ ■ ■ ■ ■ ■ ■ ●

(The scene opens with Camile and Janese playing together. Everything seems to be fine until Camile starts throwing toys.)
Janese: *(Looks up from playing.)* Hey! Stop that!
Camile: *(Throws a toy at Janese.)* Take that!
Janese: Ouch! *(She begins to cry.)* That really hurts.
Camile: *(Rushes over to Janese and gently pats her.)* I'm really sorry. I didn't mean to hurt you. Are you OK?
Janese: *(Cries harder.)* It hurts so bad! Why did you throw that at me?
Camile: *(Straightens up.)* Because I was mad!
Janese: *(Begins calming down but sniffles as she talks.)* But what did I do?
Camile: *(Picks up a toy.)* I'm so mad I could just scream and throw this through the window! *(She raises the toy above her head.)*
Janese: Stop! Stop! Didn't you hear me? I got hurt the last time you threw something, and I still don't know why you're so mad.
Camile: *(Puts down the toy and sighs.)* I'm not mad at you, Janese.
Janese: *(Wipes her brow.)* Whew! Am I ever glad to hear that! *(Turns to*

the audience.) But yikes, what would she do to me if she really were mad at me? Now that's a scary thought!

Camile: I'm mad at God.

Janese: At God? Why? I didn't know anyone ever got mad at God.

Camile: Well, you'd be mad at God if you were me.

Janese: Why? What did God do?

Camile: God made my mom sick. And I bet God is going to kill her.

Janese: Yikes! That's scary. What's the matter with your mom?

Camile: She gets headaches, so she sleeps a lot. Dad says I have to be very quiet. I've been really good lately, but she doesn't get better. I feel like I'll have to whisper in my house forever!

Janese: Did your dad say she's going to die?

Camile: I never asked him.

Janese: Did your mom ever says she's going to die?

Camile: I never asked her either. I just know it, though.

Janese: Maybe your mom needs someone to cheer her up.

Camile: Yeah, I wish I could help.

Janese: I bet you can!

Camile: How?

Janese: Let's ask these children if they have some ideas. *(Both puppets look toward the audience for ideas.)* What could we do?

(Interact with the audience. Ask follow-up questions if possible.)

Camile: Those are great ideas! I like the idea of bringing my mom some flowers. Do you know where we can get some?

Janese: I'll be right back. I know just the place. *(Janese leaves the stage and comes back with a bouquet of flowers.)*

Camile: Perfect. Let's go now!

(The two exit the stage. Have the mom enter and lie in a corner, partially covered with a blanket. There's a knock.)

Camile's Mom: *(In a weak voice)* Who is it? *(Camile and Janese enter.)*

Camile: It's me, Mom. And I brought Janese.

Camile's Mom: That's nice.

Camile: Mom, we brought you some flowers. *(She holds them out to her mom.)*

Camile's Mom: *(Sits up.)* Oh, Camile and Janese! They're beautiful! How nice!

Camile: Mom, I've been really worried. You're sick a lot. Are you going to die?

Camile's Mom: *(Laughs.)* No. I'm not dying, although sometimes it may seem that way. I just have a virus that keeps coming back right when I seem to get well. The doctor says it will just take time, but I will get well. I'm not going to die.

Camile: Really? *(She jumps up and down.)* That's great news!

Camile's Mom: But the best news of all is that you came and told me what you were worried about. It's good to talk to Dad and me when you're worried, and it's also good to talk to God. I'm really proud of you.

Camile: And I'm proud of you, Mom. *(Camile hugs her mom.)*

Camile's Mom: Why?

Camile: Because now I won't have to be quiet for the rest of my life! *(Everyone giggles as the curtain falls.)*

PUPPET SCRIPT 2

PARTY TIME!

Theme: Worship

Scripture: "Clap your hands, all you people. Shout to God with joy. The Lord Most High is wonderful. He is the great King over all the earth!" (Psalm 47:1-2).

Synopsis: Laurie and Tuni worship God after grappling with Tuni's questions.

Characters:
Laurie—a girl with a creative spark
Tuni—Laurie's friend

Props: A daisy and a bunch of inflated balloons

Tuni: *(Picks petals off a daisy and throws them into the audience.)* God loves me. God loves me not. God loves me. God...
Laurie: *(Appears on the scene and interrupts Tuni.)* What are you doing?
Tuni: *(Stops picking the petals.)* Trying to find out if God loves me or not.
Laurie: Why are you doing that?
Tuni: Because I want to know. *(She starts picking the petals again.)* God loves me. God loves me not. God loves...
Laurie: *(Interrupting)* But of course God loves you. You don't have to pick petals off a daisy to figure that out.
Tuni: Oh, yeah? How do you know?
Laurie: I just do.
Tuni: Has God ever told you?
Laurie: Well, no.
Tuni: Have you ever gotten a valentine from God on Valentine's Day?
Laurie: Uh, no.
Tuni: Have you ever gotten a birthday present from God?

Laurie: No, but...

Tuni: *(Interrupting)* Have you ever gotten a hug? How about a letter? Did you ever get invited to go somewhere with God?

Laurie: *(Waves her arms for Tuni to stop.)* Stop! Stop! Stop! And the answers are: No! No! No! But I still know God loves me.

Tuni: How?

Laurie: Because the sun rises every morning, and the sun sets each evening.

Tuni: So?

Laurie: And I know God loves me because my parents love me and care about me. They tell me about God and how much God loves me. But do you know what?

Tuni: What?

Laurie: Even if I didn't have a mom and dad to love me and tell me about God, I would still know that God loves me.

Tuni: How?

Laurie: Because the Bible tells me how much God loves me. I don't need anyone else to tell me. I just know. And I bet these kids out here have other reasons they know God loves them.

Tuni: Tell me!

(Encourage the audience to respond. Have the puppets repeat what the audience says.)

Laurie: See!

Tuni: Wow! This is great! Let's throw a party for God! Everybody, stand up!

Laurie: OK, everybody, repeat after me and do what I do. Let's celebrate God with Psalm 47:1-2: "Clap your hands, all you people."

(Clap three times. Then lead the children in repeating the words and clapping.)

Tuni: "Shout to God with loud songs of joy."

(Shout "hooray" three times. Then lead the children in repeating the words and shouting "hooray" three times.)

Laurie: "For the Lord, the Most High, is awesome."

(Jump in the air three times while shouting "awesome." Then lead the children in repeating the words and actions.)

Tuni: "A great king over all the earth!"

(Stretch arms out wide. Then lead the children in repeating the words and action.)

Laurie: Now let's really celebrate God.

(Pull out the balloons and bat them into the crowd of children. Encourage children to bat the balloons and say, "God, you're awesome! God, you're awesome!")

HELPFUL WORDS, HURTFUL WORDS

Theme: Communication

Scripture: "A gentle answer will calm a person's anger, but an unkind answer will cause more anger" (Proverbs 15:1).

Synopsis: Louie badmouths everyone he sees.

Characters:
Louie—an obnoxious boy
James—a sensitive boy
Liza—a girl who knows Louie and James

Props: A Bible

●　●　●　●　●　●　●　●　●

(The scene opens with Louie spouting off about how awful everyone is.)
Louie: *(Paces across the puppet stage in a fast, angry manner.)* What a lousy day! Can you believe it? It was supposed to be sunny, but it's cloudy. It was supposed to be warm, but it's cold. My mom said I'm supposed to clean my room, but I hate that. My teacher wants me to stay inside the lines when I color, but I don't want to do that. I want my mom to clean my room, and I want my teacher to leave me alone. Everybody is so icky!
Liza: *(Enters the stage humming.)*
Louie: And you! You're a girl! Yech! Why can't you leave me alone?
Liza: I'm not bothering you.
Louie: Oh, yes, you are. You're looking at me. And, ick, now you're talking to me.
Liza: *(Starts humming and trying to ignore Louie.)*
Louie: Oh, no, you can't ignore me. Your ugly face keeps bugging me.
Liza: What? *(She starts to cry.)*
Louie: *(Laughs.)* And now your face is really ugly and all puckered up

with those tears. What a crybaby you are!

Liza: *(Starts crying harder.)*

Louie: I'm leaving. I'm not wasting my time with an ugly crybaby.

Liza: *(Cries harder. James enters.)*

James: Liza, is that you?

Liza: *(Hides her face and tries to hide her crying.)*

James: Liza, it is you! Are you OK?

Liza: *(Hides her face while she speaks.)* Don't look at me. I'm just an ugly crybaby.

James: No, you're not. Who told you that? You just look really sad. Are you OK?

Liza: *(Lifts up her head as she sniffles.)* Louie was picking on me. He says I'm a crybaby.

James: Do you believe that?

Liza: Well, he thinks I am.

James: I don't think so. God made you a wonderful person, and I think God would be sad if God heard you talking like this.

Liza: Really? *(Brightens up.)* You really think I'm OK?

James: Yep! Because God made you. And I'm OK because God made me!

Liza: Wow! That's neat. Thanks, James. I feel better.

James: Well, I gotta run. See ya, Liza. *(He exits the stage.)*

Liza: Boy, I feel great. Now, if that Louie comes back, I'm going to call him names. I'm going to hit him. I'm going to make him cry. I can't wait 'til I see him. *(Turns to the audience.)* Don't you think that's a great idea?

(Have Liza interact with the audience. If the audience agrees, have Liza question that and lead the children to eventually say that her idea isn't a good one.)

Liza: I guess if God made me that must mean God made Louie. Ooo! Yuck! How could God make Louie? You know, Louie deserves for me to be mean to him. *(Pauses for a moment.)* But maybe I should read my Bible, huh? *(Pulls out a Bible.)* Here's what Proverbs 15:1 says: "A gentle answer will calm a person's anger, but an unkind answer will cause more anger."

Louie: *(Enters the stage.)* Hey, it's that crybaby again. What are you doing, crybaby?

Liza: Reading my Bible.

Louie: What a waste of time!

Liza: Actually, it's not. I'm learning a lot.

Louie: You mean, how to be a better crybaby?

Liza: Nope. I'm learning how to be a better Christian.

Louie: A crybaby Christian?

Liza: A better Christian. Say, I don't like how you've been calling me names. You must be really sad to say all those mean things. You must be having a bad day. I'm sorry.

Louie: Leave me alone.

Liza: You're the one who's been talking to me, so I thought it would be good if I found out what's bothering you. Maybe I can help.

Louie: Help? *(Pointing to himself)* You want to help me? *(Turns to the audience.)* Yikes! What's the matter with her? I'm getting out of here. *(He runs off the stage.)*

Liza: Hey, maybe I should read my Bible more often. *(Turns to the audience.)* What do you think?

(Allow children to respond.)

Liza: That's just what I'm going to do. Hey, I gotta go. I've got a lot of reading to do.

PUPPET SCRIPT 4

HELPING HANDS

Theme: Service

Scripture: "Then Jesus said, 'Which one of these three men do you think was a neighbor to the man who was atttacked by robbers?' The expert on the law answered, 'The one who showed him mercy.' Jesus said to him, 'Then go and do what he did' " (Luke 10:36-37).

Synopsis: Laura helps Julie when she struggles with school.

Characters:
Julie—a struggling student
Laura—a classmate
Mrs. Andrews—the teacher

Props: A book

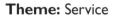

(The scene opens with Julie trying to read a book.)

Julie: *(Holding the book)* This is so hard. I hate reading! *(She turns the book upside down.)* Maybe this will be easier!

Sounds from backstage of various children's voices: Hey! There's the dummy! You mean the girl who can't read? Yeah, her. She's quite a reader—NOT! *(Then laughter.)*

Julie: *(Turns to the audience.)* Do you hear that? They're talking about me! Everybody thinks I'm so stupid. I hate reading.

Laura: *(Enters the stage.)* Hey, Julie, how are you doing?

Julie: Terrible.

Laura: What are you doing? Isn't that a hard way to read?

Julie: Every way is hard. Upside down. Right side up. Backward. Forward. They're all the same. I just can't do it.

Laura: Oh, Julie, don't give up so fast.

Julie: But they're calling me names!

Laura: Who?

Julie: Everybody! I hate being called a bad reader.

Laura: Here, let me help you. *(She picks up the book.)* Here, what's this word?

Julie: Th-th-th. I don't know. I give up.

Laura: But you haven't even read one word.

Julie: I know. It's too hard.

Laura: Here. *(She hands the book to Julie.)* Let me see what I can do. *(She exits, then returns with Mrs. Andrews, the teacher.)*

Mrs. Andrews: Hi, Julie. Laura tells me you're having trouble reading.

Julie: Oh, Mrs. Andrews. I'm just a bad reader, just like everybody says.

Mrs. Andrews: That's not true. We'll figure this out. *(She and Julie begin sharing a book and working in the background.)*

Laura: *(Speaks to the audience.)* Jesus told the story of the good Samaritan who helped the person who was robbed and lying in the road. Now, Julie isn't bleeding or lying in the road, but she's still having trouble. When have you helped people who were in trouble?

(Have Laura interact with children in the audience.)

Laura: The Bible says we're supposed to help people, but I don't think I'm being much help. I can't help Julie read.

Mrs. Andrews: *(Moves toward Laura.)* But you **are** helping Julie read. I can tell that Julie needs some testing. I think she has a problem that keeps her from learning to read. We'll be able to help Julie read. And without you, Julie may not have gotten the help she needs.

Julie: Thanks, Laura. I feel better now. I'm finding out that I'm not stupid. Thanks for helping me. *(She gives Laura a big hug.)*

PUPPET SCRIPT 5

SIBLING SQUABBLES

Theme: Fighting

Scripture: "He will settle arguments among the nations and will make decisions for many nations. Then they will make their swords into plows and their spears into hooks for trimming trees. Nations will no longer fight other nations, nor will they train for war anymore" (Isaiah 2:4).

Synopsis: Brothers Jason and Joshua fight about everything.

Characters:
Jason—the older brother
Joshua—the younger brother
Father—Jason and Joshua's dad

Props: A toy truck

* * * * * * * * * *

(The scene opens with Jason and Joshua squabbling.)
Jason: *(Grabs a truck from Joshua.)* Hey, that's mine.
Joshua: *(Races toward Jason.)* No, it's mine!
Jason: *(Pulls the truck.)* It's mine.
Joshua: You took it from me. Give it back now.
Jason: *(Runs off the stage.)* Mine! Mine! Mine!
Joshua: Hey! Bring that back right now. *(Turns to talk to the audience.)* Brothers! Don't they drive you crazy sometimes? Mine sure does. Sometimes brothers and sisters are sure hard to live with. Oh, no, I hear Jason coming back again.
Jason: *(Skips onto the stage with the truck.)* Hey, Joshua, do you like my truck?
Joshua: That's not your truck. That's my truck.
Jason: It's mine!
Joshua: No! It's mine.

Father: *(Enters.)* What's all this noise?

Joshua: Jason took my truck.

Jason: But it's mine.

Father: Give me the truck. *(Jason reluctantly gives it to him.)* Why can't the two of you get along? The Bible tells us that it's not good to fight.

Jason: Sorry, Dad.

Joshua: Yeah, sorry.

Father: *(Leaving the stage)* I hope that settles everything.

Jason: Hey, Joshua, do you want to sing a song with me?

Joshua: Sure. Which one?

Jason: How about "Jesus Loves Me"?

Joshua: I'm tired of that song. How about "The B-I-B-L-E"?

Jason: No. I want to sing "Jesus Loves Me."

Joshua: We always sing that song. How about "Father Abraham"?

Jason: *(Getting louder)* No! I want "Jesus Loves Me."

Joshua: *(Shouting)* No!

Jason: *(Louder)* Yes!

Joshua: *(Louder)* No!

Father: *(Runs onto the stage.)* Now what?

Jason: Joshua won't sing "Jesus Loves Me" with me.

Joshua: Jason won't cooperate.

Father: You're fighting over which church song to sing? *(Turns to the audience.)* Can you believe this? Isaiah 2 says that someday there won't be any more war. I wish that day were today, but here I am in the middle of a huge family war! Maybe you all can help. What do you think these two can do to get along better?

(Have the audience share their ideas. Have the father puppet repeat the ideas as if he's considering how to help his sons get along together.)

Father: Those were all good ideas. But until you boys can play together nicely, I think Jason should play over here. *(He points to one side of the stage.)* And Joshua should play over here. *(He points to the opposite side of the stage.)* Why does being a father have to be so hard sometimes? *(Exits.)*

Joshua: *(Playing alone)* Hey, Jason, what are you doing?

Jason: *(Playing alone)* Nothing. What about you?

Joshua: Nothing. Do you like doing nothing all by yourself?

Jason: Nope. Do you?

Joshua: Nope.

Jason: Do you think we could play together?

Joshua: As long as we don't fight. I wish we didn't fight so much.

Jason: Yeah, me, too. I guess I just get carried away sometimes.

Joshua: Yeah, I guess I do, too.

Jason: Do you think God is mad at us?

Joshua: Not if we say we're sorry, and we try not to fight.

Jason: Let's try to make God happy.

Joshua: That would make me happy.

Jason: So where's that truck?

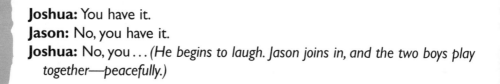

Joshua: You have it.

Jason: No, you have it.

Joshua: No, you . . . *(He begins to laugh. Jason joins in, and the two boys play together—peacefully.)*

JUST ME

Theme: Loneliness

Scripture: "How long will you forget me, Lord? Forever? How long will you hide from me?" (Psalm 13:1).

Synopsis: Susie feels left out and alone.

Characters:
Susie—a girl who feels abandoned
Kathy—Susie's peer
Mom—Susie's mom

Props: A Bible

▶ ● ● ● ● ● ● ● ●

(The scene opens with Susie playing unhappily by herself.)

Susie: *(Pacing across the stage and periodically looking into the audience)* Oh, I'm bored, bored, bored. There's nothing to do.

Mom: *(Appears on the stage and rushes by in a hurry.)* Hi, Susie. I hope you're having fun.

Susie: *(Tries to catch her.)* Will you play with me?

Mom: *(Leaving the stage)* Gotta run. I have to cook and clean and get the laundry done. Later, Susie. Later.

Susie: *(Sits down, frustrated.)* There's nothing to do, and there's nobody to do it with.

Kathy: *(Enters the stage.)* Hey, Susie. What are you doing?

Susie: *(Doesn't look up because she's so frustrated.)* Nothin'.

Kathy: That's too bad. I gotta get to ballet class. See you later. *(She leaves the stage.)*

Susie: *(Looks up and then gets up to go after Kathy.)* Hey, wait. Don't you have time to play? Wait! Wait! *(Then she turns around and sits down again, feeling rejected.)* Kathy doesn't even have time for me. What can I do? *(Pauses and thinks for a moment.)* I know, maybe I could play softball for a while. I could catch fly balls. *(She pretends to catch a ball.)* I could strike out the best of the batters. *(She pretends to throw a pitch. She pretends to pick up a bat and swing it a few times.)* I could hit home runs. *(She swings her imaginary bat.)* But, hey. *(She becomes sullen and puts down the imaginary bat.)* No one is here to throw me a pitch. I can't play softball alone. *(She sits down again.)* Does anybody have any ideas for what I could do? *(Turns to the audience and solicits the children's ideas. Have Susie try a few ideas and be enthusiastic at first. Then have her get frustrated because it's lonely playing alone.)* Oh, well. At least I tried. Is there anything else I could do? *(Pauses and thinks for a while.)* I know; maybe the Bible has something to say. *(Turns to the audience.)* What do you think of that idea? *(Allow children to participate. Then have Susie get a Bible.)* I wonder if God knows how I feel. *(Looks up into the sky.)* Hey, God, I'm not very happy right now. Nobody will play with me. There's nothing to do. I feel like no one has any time for me. Do you have time for me? *(Pauses and then looks into the audience.)* Even God is pretty quiet. Do you think God is too busy? *(Opens up the Bible.)* Everyone has always told me that God talks to us through the Bible. Maybe I should find out what God has to say. *(Pauses as she looks at a page.)* Oh, here's something: "How long will you forget me, Lord? Forever? How long will you hide from me?" That's in the Bible? There it is: Psalm 13:1. I can't believe this is in here. This is exactly how I feel. Wow, it must be OK to feel lonely and forgotten. *(Closes the Bible and looks up.)* Hey, thanks, God. I guess I thought I should talk to you only when I'm happy and when I want to praise you. I didn't think it was very Christian to feel sad, mad, or lonely. I guess it's OK to have those feelings, too.

Mom: *(Enters the stage.)* Hey, Susie, I'm finished with my chores. Do you want to play—or are you busy?

Susie: *(Holds the Bible close.)* Actually, I've been kind of busy talking to God.

Mom: I think that's terrific. Do you want me to come back later?

Susie: Nope. Let's play Catch.

Kathy: *(Enters the stage.)* Hey, Susie, what are you up to?

Susie: My mom and I are going to play Catch.

Kathy: Can I play, too? Ballet class is over, and I don't have anyone to play with.

Susie: You can play Catch with us.

Kathy: Great! I like it when I have someone to play with.

Susie: Me, too. *(She puts her arm around Kathy's shoulders, and they exit the stage happily.)*

PUPPET SCRIPT 7

HAPPINESS IS

Theme: Happiness

Scripture: "Sing, Jerusalem. Israel, shout for joy! Jerusalem, be happy and rejoice with all your heart" (Zephaniah 3:14).

Synopsis: Nancy and Andrew name everything that makes them happy.

Characters:
 Nancy—a sixth-grader
 Andrew—a kindergartner

Props: A stick

(The scene opens with Andrew drawing pictures in the sand with a stick.)
Andrew: *(Hums a song as he draws pictures in the sand with a stick.)*
Nancy: *(Enters the stage.)* Hi, Andrew! What are you doing?
Andrew: I'm drawing pictures.
Nancy: Fun! What kind of pictures?
Andrew: I'm drawing pictures of everything that makes me happy.
Nancy: *(Giggles.)* Are you sure you have enough sand?
Andrew: *(Stops drawing, thinks for a minute, and then giggles.)* Let's see if we can fill up all the sand with pictures.
Nancy: That will be fun because this is a huge ocean beach!
Andrew: Let's try it!
Nancy: OK. Let's draw a picture of an elephant.
Andrew: Popcorn.
Nancy: Swings.
Andrew: Purple pants.
Nancy: Polka dots.
Andrew: Balloons.
Nancy: Rainbows.

Andrew: *(Turning to the audience)* What about you? What ideas do you have? What makes you happy?

(Allow children to name things that make them happy. Nancy and Andrew can then name other items if the children need ideas. Treat this as a brainstorming time.)

Nancy: Wow, we really have a lot of great ideas.

Andrew: Yeah. God sure gives us a lot of things that make us happy.

Nancy: We really have a great God.

Andrew: Even the Bible tells us how great God is. In Zephaniah, it says to sing, shout, and rejoice because God is with us.

Nancy: Why don't we sing, shout, and rejoice?

Andrew: What a great idea! In fact, that idea makes me happy! We can add that to our list of happy things.

Nancy: I know! Let's sing a song to God—just like the Bible says. *(She looks at the audience.)* Come on, everybody! Stand up. Let's all sing together.

Andrew: Let's sing "Jingle Bells."

Nancy: But it's not Christmastime.

Andrew: I mean, let's sing these words to the tune of "Jingle Bells." I'll show you: "God, you're great! God, you're great! We worship you today. You give us so many things—you're great in every way. Hey, God, you're great! God, you're great! We worship you today. You give us so many things—you're great in every way!"

Nancy: Let's sing.

(Have everyone sing together.)

Andrew: You know what, Nancy?

Nancy: What?

Andrew: That singing made me happy.

Nancy: Me, too, Andrew. Me, too.

MY SHOES, YOUR SHOES

Theme: Giving

Scripture: "Then a poor widow came and put in two small copper coins, which were only worth a few cents. Calling his followers to him, Jesus said, 'I tell you the truth, this poor widow gave more than all those rich people. They gave only what they did not need. This woman is very poor, but she gave all she had; she gave all she had to live on' " (Mark 12:42-44).

Synopsis: At a homeless shelter, Steve surprises everyone with his gift.

Characters:
Steve—a volunteer at a homeless shelter
Dad—Steve's dad
Johnnie—a boy staying at the shelter

Props: A pair of tennis shoes

• • • • • • • • • •

(The scene opens with Steve and his dad at a homeless shelter getting ready to serve a meal.)

Steve: I'm glad we do this, Dad. You know, I think God likes what we're doing.

Dad: I agree. When people are hungry, we should make sure they get something to eat. That's why I like helping at this homeless shelter. These people usually don't have enough to eat.

Steve: But they will tonight. We're going to make sure they get something really yummy.

Dad: You bet.

Steve: Hey, it looks like the meal is ready. Let's open the doors and serve it.

Dad: OK, here we go. *(He pretends to open a door.)*

Steve: Wow, there are a lot of people waiting for food today. Come on in! *(He begins to serve the meal.)*

Johnnie: *(Enters and waits for something to eat.)* Boy, that food looks good. Give me a whole bunch.

Dad: Here, we'll give you some, and then you can come back for more after everyone has had something to eat. *(Dishes out some food.)*

Johnnie: Can't I have a little bit more?

Steve: *(Whispers.)* Psst. Here. Have an extra roll, but don't tell anybody. *(Pretends to give Johnnie a roll.)*

Johnnie: *(Smiles.)* Wow. Thanks! *(He then walks over to the opposite end of the stage and begins to eat.)*

Steve: Hey, Dad, did you notice Johnnie?

Dad: Of course. He comes in here every time, and he always wants more food. And I know you'll give him an extra roll every time. *(He smiles and winks at Steve.)* How could I not notice?

Steve: I know, but did you notice his shoes? They're falling apart. It looks like the bottoms are going to fall off any minute.

Dad: It's sad, isn't it?

Steve: We've got to do something.

Dad: I wish we could, too.

Steve: Dad, in Sunday school we learned about the poor widow in Mark 12. She had hardly any money, but she still gave some. The coins were worth only a penny, but they were all she had. Jesus talked about how good it is to give what we have.

Dad: That's true.

Steve: *(Starts taking off his shoes and places them on the stage.)* I'm giving these to Johnnie.

Dad: But they're your new running shoes!

Steve: But Johnnie needs them.

Dad: Steve, we don't have the money to buy you another pair.

Steve: That's OK. I have some old ones at home. In fact, I have a closet full of shoes. Johnnie needs a new pair of shoes more than I do. *(He walks over to Johnnie.)*

Johnnie: Hi, Steve.

Steve: Hi, Johnnie. I thought you might like to have these. *(Hands the shoes to Johnnie.)*

Johnnie: Wow! Really? These are awesome! Can I put them on now?

Steve: Yeah, go ahead.

Johnnie: *(Putting on the shoes)* Hey, these are great! Thanks! *(Johnnie jumps for joy, then skips offstage.)* I can't wait to show everybody.

Steve: *(Walks back toward his dad.)* Boy, that sure made my day.

Dad: I'm glad you decided to share what you have with Johnnie. I'm proud of you, Steve. And I know God is proud of you, too.

SECTION 3: CHILDREN'S WORSHIP SERVICES

Why have children's worship services? Shouldn't kids worship in the regular church service?

In a recent survey of children's ministers, respondents to that question split down the middle. Fifty percent of the children's pastors said children should always worship with adults. The other 50 percent said children need their own age-appropriate worship service.

This book is for those who offer worship services for children. Children need to encounter God through experiences and language they can understand if they are to fully experience their faith. The worship services in this book will help children do exactly that. These services will prompt your children to go beyond just learning about God, learning about the Bible, and learning about being a Christian. Your children will experience the living God—and they'll be changed by their encounter.

Use these worship services to

● **periodically replace existing children's church services to breathe new life into your curriculum.**

● **"get the feel" of what it means to lead children in age-appropriate worship.** Once you catch on, use the worship ingredients in Section 1 of this book to create more worship services.

As you lead children in worship, remember to

● **help children understand that God is their audience in children's worship.** Everything they do should be focused on God—not on their performance. Encourage them to sing songs *to* God; to offer praise *to* God, and even to giggle *to* God.

● **be a role model.** Don't just tell children what to do and then step aside. Kids will learn a great deal about worship by watching how you worship. When your group sings, let kids see you singing to God also.

● **enter into these services prayerfully.** Worship can be one of the most spiritually enriching experiences we have as Christians. It shouldn't be too strictly programmed or manipulated. Spend time in prayer, asking God to infuse everything that's done with God's presence. Throughout the services, focus on God rather than on your outline.

TOGETHER FOREVER

Theme: God's family

Scriptures: Hebrews 10:19-25 and Philippians 2:1-5

Preparation: You'll need a Bible, a telephone cord, a blindfold, masking tape, and a towel.

In this worship service the children will celebrate togetherness. They'll sing songs together, pray together, and learn together. The children will see that being a part of God's family is fun and rewarding—that God's family is a place of love and belonging. And they'll learn ways to stay close to other Christians and to God.

THE SERVICE

1 **Responding to God with creative movement**—Say: **Today we're going to celebrate being part of God's family. Let's have fun being part of God's big, happy family.**

Have children skip around the room. When you shout "together," have each child find a partner to skip with. When you shout "together" again, have each pair find another pair to skip with. Continue until you have a large group skipping together. Say: **Let's skip together as one large group and say, "God, we love to be in your family!"**

Have the children stop skipping. Say: **Each of us is an important part of God's family. There are lots of things that God's family does.** Ask:

● **What do the members of God's family do?**

● **What is your job in God's family?**

Say: **As members of God's family, we do some things by ourselves. We also do some things with other people. God has important tasks for all of us to do.**

2 **Responding to God with music**—Have the children stand while they sing the song below.

Sing the song through once or twice to teach children the words. Then sing it a third time. This time, when the children sing the word "you," have them each find a partner, stand face to face, and point toward heaven. When the next "you" comes along, have each child find another partner and repeat the motion. Sing slowly and pause for children to find partners.

Sing these words to the tune of "Twinkle, Twinkle, Little Star":
We're a family with you, God.
It's great to be loved by you.
You care for us, this is true,
When we're happy, when we're blue.
We're a family with you, God.
It's great to be loved by you.

3 **Responding to God with Scripture**—You'll need a long, coiled, stretchy phone cord from a wall phone. (Unplug the cord from the headset and the actual phone.) Have the children stand in a circle and hold onto the phone cord. If you have more than 10 children, bring more than one phone cord and form more circles.

Read aloud Hebrews 10:19-25. Then say: **Let's talk about this Scripture. Hebrews 10 tells us how to be God's family. Whenever I say the word "far," walk backward and stretch as far apart as you can without letting go of the telephone cord. Hang on tight so you don't drop it. When I say the word "near," come as close together as you can. Be careful not to pull too hard on the phone cord. Let's begin.**

Hebrews 10 says we have been brought near (pause so children can move close together) **to God because Jesus died for us on the cross. And because of this we can try to stay far** (pause so children can move far apart) **from evil and bad things.** Ask:

● **What are some evil things that we want to be far away from?** Say: **God wants us to stay near** (pause so children can move close together) **to God.** Ask:

● **How do we stay near to God?**

Say: **Also, it's not good to get too far** (pause so children can move far apart) **from God.** Ask:

● **How do we become far away from God?**

Say: **The Bible also talks about relationships between people. God wants us to love each other and to be near** (pause so children can move close together) **one another.**

● **Why is it good to stay close to people?**

● **What can we do to stay close to other people?**

Even if we're far (pause so children can move far apart) **from each other, we can still be near** (pause as children move close together) **in spirit.**

- **How can we be close in spirit when we're far apart from each other?**

Have children stop moving in and out. Say: **Since we are all part of God's family, we need to stay close to each other and to God even when we're physically far away. Thanks for all your good ideas on how to stay close to each other. Let's thank God for including us in God's family.**

4 Responding to God with prayer—Have children stand in a circle. Say: **Think about one thing you like about being in God's family. When everyone has thought of an idea, we'll begin our prayer.**

Pause to allow the children time to think of ideas. Ask the children to put their hands together as if praying to show that they have an idea and are ready to pray.

Tell the class your idea by completing this sentence prayer: **God, I like being in your family because . . .** After your prayer, link arms with the child on your right. Have that child complete the sentence prayer and link arms with the next child to the right. Continue until everyone has completed the sentence prayer and has linked arms. Have the children squeeze close together as they say "amen."

5 Responding to God with creative movement—Say: **Now let's explore what we can do as members of God's family.**

Stand in a circle with the children. Have children imitate your actions as you speak the words.

Say: **God, we are here together, thankful to you for giving us ourselves** (hug yourself) **and each other** (clasp your hands). **Thank you for feet** (touch your foot) **that walk, run, and carry us places. Thank you for knees** (touch your knees) **that don't buckle when we're afraid. Thank you for ears** (touch your ears) **to hear your Word. Thank you for noses** (touch your nose) **to smell the sweet scents that surround us. We appreciate our mouths** (touch your mouth) **to talk to each other and for our heads** (touch your head) **to think and to wonder. Thank you for eyes** (touch your eye) **to see the many things you've made and for our hands** (touch your hands) **to help each other. We love being part of your family.** (Initiate a group hug.)

6 Message—Before the service, lay out a masking tape path on the floor around the room. Add several curves.

Have the children sit in chairs or on the floor.

Read aloud Philippians 2:1-5. As you read, have the children call out "yes" in answer to each of the questions in the first verse.

Blindfold one child. Have the rest of the children scatter along the masking tape path. Have the blindfolded child attempt to find his or her way along the path. Have the first child along the path guide the blindfolded child on the path to the second child. Continue having the children help the blindfolded child until he or she reaches the end of the path. Then take off the blindfold and have the children sit down. If you have time, have other children take turns being blindfolded and led along the path. Ask:

- **How did it feel to be guided along the path?**
- **How did it feel to guide your friends along the path?**

Read Philippians 2:1-5 again. Ask:

- **How do Christians show they're interested in others?**
- **What can you do to serve others in God's family?**

Say: **It's good to do whatever we can to help each other. You showed your concern for one another when you gently guided your friends along the path. You made sure that your friends didn't get hurt. We can do the same for all the members of God's family. When we serve each other, we please God.**

7 **Responding to God by giving**—Say: **Let's take our offering to God together.**

Have children stand around a towel and hold it taut horizontally. One by one, have the children put their offerings on the towel. Then have the group carry the towel to your altar area.

8 **Responding to God with music**—Say: **Let's sing a song about togetherness.** Sing these words to the tune of "Three Blind Mice":

To-geth-er. To-geth-er.
That's what we are.
That's what we are.
Together we praise and thank our God.
Together we worship and sing to God.
Together we're part of God's family.
To-geth-er. Wow!

After children learn the song, say: **Now let's add some actions to the song to show that we want to link up with each other and worship and serve God together.**

Form pairs and have partners link up in new ways each time they sing the word "together." For example, a pair could do the following actions:

To-ge-ther. (Hold hands.)
To-ge-ther. (Put feet together.)
That's what we are.
That's what we are.
Together (stand hip to hip) **we praise and thank our God.**
Together (put knees together) **we worship and sing to God.**
Together (put elbows together) **we're part of God's family.**
To-geth-er. (Put ears together.) **Wow!**

Form new pairs and sing the song again. Have the new pairs find new ways to link together.

9 **Responding to God with the closing**—Say: **Each of us is a special and valued member of God's family. Let's find out how each of you is special.**

Have the children form a circle, then ask one child to stand in the middle. Have the rest of the group say, "We're together as a family for (child's name)." Mention one way the child in the middle of the circle can contribute to God's family. For example, you might say that Emily helps everyone rejoice in the Lord. Then have the group give the child a group hug. Have the children form a big circle again.

Have another child go to the middle of the circle. Tell one way that child can contribute to God's family, then have the group repeat the sentence and give him or her a group hug. Repeat this process until every child has been hugged.

Then have the children spread their arms wide to give God a big cheer as they say, "Thanks, God, for making us part of your family!"

10 **Responding to God with prayer**—Say: **Let's worship God in prayer together.** Ask:
* **Why do we worship God?**

Have children stand in a circle, hold their hands out toward the middle of the circle, and grasp hands. Explain that each time you say, "We worship you," children are to raise their clasped hands high. When you say anything else, they should drop their hands low.

Pray: **God, thank you for this time together.** (Hands low.) **We worship you.** (Hands high.) **We sing songs to you.** (Hands low.) **We worship you.** (Hands high.) **We hear your Word and learn more about you.** (Hands low.) **We worship you.** (Hands high.) **In church** (hands low) **we worship you.** (Hands high.) **As children** (hands low) **we worship you.** (Hands high.) **Together as a family** (hands low) **we worship you.** (Hands high.) **Amen.**

THOSE BAD, BAD DAYS

Theme: Bad day

Scripture: Micah 1:8 and John 16:20, 22b

Preparation: You'll need a whistle, a glove or mitten, newsprint, masking tape, and markers.

In this worship service, the children will talk about what it's like to have bad days. The children will discover that everyone has bad days sometimes. But they'll find out that even on the worst days, God is still with us and God is still worthy of our praise. Have fun helping children learn to cope with "those bad, bad days."

THE SERVICE

1 Responding to God with creative movement—Say: **Today we're talking about bad days. We've all had bad days. Think of something that can make your whole day go badly. For example, once . . .** Tell the children about something that caused you to have a bad day, such as the time you left your snow boots outside overnight during a blizzard and you had to dump the snow out and wear cold boots to work.

When the children have each thought of at least one idea, have them act sad by shuffling around the room with their heads down and their bottom lips sticking out. Tell children that each time you blow the whistle they should pair up with someone and tell that person one thing that causes them to have a bad day. After each child has shared, the pairs should then say, "What a baaaaa—d day" (like a sheep).

Then have the children start shuffling again until you blow the whistle. Continue until children have paired up with several different children.

Then say: **We can do more than tell just each other about our** troubles. There's someone else who wants to listen, too. Can you guess who?

2 Responding to God with music—Say: **Jesus knows that all of us have bad days sometimes. He wants us to tell him about everything—even things that aren't happy. So let's sing a song and tell Jesus all about our troubles.**

Sing this song to the tune of "Baa, Baa, Black Sheep":

Oh, dear Jesus, it's a bad day.
Will it end or will it stay?
Nothing went right, not a thing.
We're unhappy as we sing.
Oh, dear Jesus, it's a bad day.
Will it end or will it stay?

As soon as the children are familiar with the words, have them think of actions to go along with the words.

3 Responding to God with Scripture—Say: **People in the Bible had bad days, too. Listen while I read about how sad Micah was.**

Read Micah 1:8. Say: **Let's act out what Micah did when he was sad. Then we'll think of other ways to act sad.**

Play Micah Says, a version of Simon Says. Have one child be "Micah," who leads the other children in sad actions. This is how the game works: If Micah says, "Micah says, 'Cry like a wild dog,' " the children should cry and howl like a dog. But if Micah says, "Jump for joy," the children shouldn't jump for joy because it's not a sad action and because Micah didn't say, "Micah says, 'Jump for joy.' "

Encourage children to include motions from the Scripture, such as making sad sounds like the owls do, walking barefoot, moaning, or crying. Also encourage them to include actions from their own lives, such as pouting or curling up in a small, sad ball.

Have several children take turns being Micah. Then stop the game and have the children sit down. Ask:

● **How do we act when bad things happen to us?**
● **Does crying and pouting make the bad things go away?**
● **Why do we act the way we do?**

Say: **Sometimes our actions help things get better. For example, crying can make some of the hurt go away. But sometimes our actions just make things worse. For example, it's not a good idea to start hitting people when we're having a bad day, because that will only get us into more trouble.**

It's OK to act sad when we have bad days. But we also need to remember to ask God and others for help so our bad days can turn into good days. Let's ask God for help right now.

4 Responding to God with prayer—Have children sit in a circle. Say: **Let's tell God about the bad things that happened this week. Bad things slow us down like running over rocks without our shoes on. As we tell about the things that happened, let's take off our shoes.**

Have the child on your right name one bad thing that happened to him or her in the past week by completing this sentence: "God, this week..."

After naming one bad thing, have the child take off one shoe and place it in the middle of the circle.

Then have the next child repeat the process. Continue until everyone is wearing only one shoe.

Then begin the process again, starting with the child on your left and continuing around the circle to the left. Have each child take off his or her remaining shoe and add it to the pile in the middle of the circle.

Keep the shoes in a pile while children remain in their socks or barefoot for the next few activities.

End the prayer by saying with the children: **Hear our prayer, O God. Amen.**

Say: **Without our shoes, we're stuck because it hurts our feet to go without shoes. Sometimes when bad days happen, we get stuck, too. Let's experience what happens during a bad day.**

5 Responding to God with creative movement—Have children stand in a circle and follow your motions as you say: **Sometimes when we have a bad day, we run away as fast as we can** (turn around and run quickly in place) **or sometimes we just stop** (stay still) **because we don't know what to do. Sometimes we want to curl up in a ball** (sit down and draw your feet in toward your body) **and wish everyone and everything would go away** (hide your face in your knees). **But, God, even when things get bad, you want us to keep going** (jump up and move your feet) **and reach high when we feel low** (extend your arms high into the air) **and reach out to others if we need help** (touch another person).

6 Message—Tape a sheet of newsprint on each of the four walls of the room. Draw a picture of a mom on one sheet, a picture of Jesus on another, a picture of children on another, and a picture of a dad on the other. You may want to paste magazine pictures onto the newsprint instead of drawing.

Say: **Listen to what the Bible says about sad times. In these verses, Jesus is telling his disciples what will happen after he dies.**

Have the children stand while you read aloud John 16:20, 22b. As you read, have children pretend to cry each time you say the word "sad." Have children cheer and smile each time you say the word "happy." Have children jump in the air each time you say the word "joy."

After you've read the Scripture, have the children sit down. Say: **Jesus' followers were sad that Jesus left them when he was crucified. But Jesus knew their sadness wouldn't last long. Jesus promised to return and make them happy again. Jesus comforted his followers when things went wrong. Let's talk about what comforts us when things go wrong.**

Say: **I'm going to read a list of bad things that sometimes happen. After I read each one, walk to the newsprint that best represents who you would go to when something like that happens.**

Read the following situations aloud one by one. Pause to allow children time to walk to the appropriate sheets of newsprint:

- **A teacher yells at you.**
- **Your dog bites you.**
- **You're mad at your mom.**
- **You don't know what to do.**
- **You're scared to walk alone.**
- **You lose your homework.**
- **You feel alone and don't have anyone to play with.**
- **Your bike chain breaks.**
- **You cut your hand.**

Gather the children and have them sit down. Ask:

- **How does your mom help you when you're having a bad day?**
- **How do your friends help you when you're having a bad day?**
- **How does your dad help you when you're having a bad day?**
- **How does Jesus help you when you're having a bad day?**

Say: **All of us have people who care about us and want to help us. Some of us may not have moms, but maybe we have good teachers or neighbors to help. Some people may not have dads to help, but they have uncles or grandfathers. Friends, family members, and Jesus are all good people to go to when we need help with a bad day. Let's thank God for those people.**

7 Responding to God with prayer—Have children squat in a circle. Have the child on your right jump up and name someone he or she talks to when a bad day comes along (such as a mom, dad, grandma, grandpa, sister, brother, teacher, or friend).

That child then squats down and the next child on the right jumps up and names a person he or she goes to. Continue until every child has named one person. Go around the circle again and have children jump up one at a time and say, "Thank you, God, for these great people!" Once everyone has done this, have the entire group jump up together and shout "amen" at the same time.

8 Responding to God by giving—Use a glove to collect the offering instead of using a collection plate. Have the children put their money inside the glove.

Before you pass the glove, say: **When we have bad days, we can let them remind us that there are some people who have a lot of bad days. Some people don't have enough to eat. Other people have never heard of Jesus. We can remember to help others who have bad days. Let's take our offering now. Put your offering inside the glove. Let the glove remind you to be a helping hand.**

After you take the offering, say: **Let's ask God for help on** *our* **bad days.**

9 **Responding to God with prayer**—Have children stand in a circle and hold hands. Explain that when you name things that happen on bad days, children should squeeze each other's hands. When you name things that happen on good days, children should relax their hands.

Then pray: **God, thank you for always being with us.** (Relax.) **Sometimes we feel sad for no reason.** (Squeeze.) **But we tell you how we feel.** (Relax.) **Sometimes people yell at us.** (Squeeze.) **Sometimes we get a smile from a friend.** (Relax.) **Sometimes we even get a hug.** (Relax.) **God, help us when we get mad.** (Squeeze.) **And cheer us on when we're happy.** (Relax.) **Help us know that even though bad days come** (squeeze)**, they will eventually go away and good days will come again.** (Relax.) **Amen.**

10 **Responding to God with music**—Have children stand in a circle around the shoes. Sing "He's Got the Whole World" once. Then have children take turns naming something that changes a bad day into a good day, such as sharing a Popsicle with a best friend or singing "Jesus Loves Me."

After a child names something, have the child search through the pile for one of his or her shoes and put it on. After all the children have put on one shoe, sing "He's Got the Whole World" again.

Then go around the circle again and have children each name a second thing that can turn a bad day into a good day. As each child shares an idea, have the child find his or her other shoe and put it on.

When the children have all shared and they all have their shoes on, sing the song one last time.

Say: **The good thing about bad days is that they don't have to stay bad days. There are lots of things we can do to change a bad day into a good one. One of the best ways is to remember that God really does have the whole world in God's hands. God takes care of us and loves us even on our worst days.**

Now that you all have your shoes back on, you're ready to face the outside world with your new ability to change bad days into good days. Let's go take on even the very worst bad days.

JOYFUL NOISES

Theme: Celebration

Scripture: Psalm 81:1-3 and Psalm 150

Preparation: You'll need one balloon for every two children, a note card and pen for each child, four rolls of different-colored crepe paper, a metal bowl, coins, and confetti.

In this worship service, the children will have fun praising God with joyful noises. They'll learn to shout, sing, pray, and give an offering with noises that please God. They'll also learn that joyful noises don't have to be loud—quiet noises can be joyful, too. Have fun praising God with sound today.

THE SERVICE

1 **Responding to God with creative movement**—Say: **Today we're talking about joyful noises, so let's get noisy while we talk about the things that bring us joy.**

Form pairs and tell children to hold both of their partners' hands. Give each pair a balloon and have the partners bounce the balloon up in the air with their connected arms. Have them shout out something they're glad God has made in each of the following categories as you call out the category name: animals, colors, movies, cartoons, food, sports, books, and school.

After a few minutes of lively play, retrieve the balloons and say: **God's creation is full of things that give us joy. Let's sing about them and make a joyful noise to God.**

2 **Responding to God with music**—Ask children to each find something in the room that makes a lot of noise that they can use as they sing a song. Children might find blocks to hit together, a toy piano, a stuffed animal that they make the animal noises for, or a pencil they can hit on a table top.

Sing a joyful song such as "Rise and Shine," "Praise Him, Praise Him," or "If You're Happy and You Know It." During the song have children make joyful noises with the things they've found.

Say: **God likes our joyful noises because they praise God. Let's praise God with a passage from the Bible.**

3 **Responding to God with Scripture**—Have children echo the words and copy your motions as you lead them in Psalm 81:1-3.
"Sing aloud (sing, "La, la")
to God our strength. (Make muscles with your arms.)
Shout out loud (shout, "Joy, joy")
to the God of Jacob. (Raise your hands in prayer toward the sky.)
Begin the music. (Sing a portion of your group's favorite song.)
Play the tambourines. (Shake your entire body.)
Play pleasant music on the harps and lyres. (Pretend to strum a harp.)
Blow the trumpet (pretend to play a trumpet and make trumpet noises)
at the time of the new moon (point to the sky)**;**
when the moon is full (howl at the moon)
when our feast begins!" (Pretend to eat.)
Have the children sit down. Ask:
● **What would you sing to God?**
● **What kind of music would you play to God?**
● **What would you praise God for?**
● **What is it like to praise God with noises?**
Say: **God has done so many great things that it's easy to get excited about how good God is. And when we get excited, sometimes we get noisy. That's great when we make a joyful noise to God. Let's praise God with prayer right now.**

4 **Responding to God with prayer**—Have children sit in a big circle, then number off, starting with one. Give each child a note card and a pen. Have them write their numbers on the cards. Have the children prop up their numbers in front of them.

Have the child who is #1 name one thing he or she likes to celebrate about God. For example, the child might say, "Praise God for making animals" or "Thank you for listening to my prayers."

Then have that child call out another number. The child with that number jumps up and switches places with #1. Then the second child says a sentence prayer praising God and calls out another child's number. Then they switch places.

Continue until every child's number has been called. As soon as a child's number has been called and the child has had a turn, have the child put the note card face down so he or she isn't called again.

When everyone has had a turn, end the prayer with everyone shouting a joyful "amen" and jumping up at the same time.

Say: **It was fun to pray out loud and make noise to God. Now let's make noise with a friend.**

5 Responding to God with creative movement—Say: **Let's make joyful noises that are loud and joyful noises that are soft. Follow my lead. If I shout, you shout, too. If I whisper, you whisper, too.**

Have children wander around the room. When you shout, "Celebrate God," have children pair up with the child nearest to them. Have each child clap hands with his or her partner twice, then together shout, "Celebrate God," while raising their hands in the air. Then have children wander around the room again. The second time, whisper, "Celebrate God," and have the children do the actions described above, except that they will whisper, not shout, "Celebrate God."

Repeat the activity five or six times. Then have the children sit down. Ask:
● **What kinds of noisy praises are there?**
● **What kinds of quiet praises are there?**

Say: **God wants us to make a joyful noise. Sometimes our noises can be noisy like when we shout, stomp, or sing. Sometimes our joyful noises are quiet like when we whisper, pray, or hum. No matter how loud or quiet we are, God is pleased when we make a joyful noise.**

6 Message—Have children sit in a tight circle. Give four children each a roll of different-colored crepe paper. Explain that as you read the Scripture, each time you say the word "praise," the children holding the crepe paper should hold one end of their crepe paper rolls and roll the crepe paper on the floor to other children in the circle. All four rolls of crepe paper will be rolling at the same time. The next time you say "praise," have the children who received the rolls hold the unrolled part in front of them and roll the crepe paper to someone else.

Read aloud Psalm 150. Pause after each "praise." Make sure that each child gets the roll of crepe paper at least once. Reread the psalm if necessary.

Together, look at the crepe-paper weaving. Ask:
● **What did the Bible say to praise God with?**
● **What else can we praise God with?**

Say: **I think we can praise God with this weaving. Look at the colors of this weaving. Think of something you can praise God for that is one of these colors. For example, I see the blue paper, and I want to praise God for the blue sky.**

Have the children think of things to praise God about that are the same colors as the paper in the weaving.

Say: **Let's make a joyful noise to God with these colors.**

Have the children pick up the ends of the crepe paper and wiggle them so the paper rustles.

Pray: **God, listen to our noise and know that we praise you for all the things that are ...** (list the colors in the weaving). **Just as the people in the Bible made a joyful noise on their instruments, we make a joyful noise to you with these beautiful colors. Amen.**

7 **Responding to God by giving**—Bring a metal bowl to collect the offering. Put the bowl on the floor and let each child stand over the bowl and drop his or her coins into it. Bring along several extra coins in case some children don't have any.

After this noisy offering has been collected, say: **This offering made a joyful noise to God. Now let's praise God with some noisy words.**

8 **Responding to God with music**—Sing these words to God to the tune of "Deep and Wide":

Jump and shout,
Jump and shout.
We all praise you
When we jump and shout.
Jump and shout,
Jump and shout.
We all praise you
When we jump and shout.

Have children actually jump whenever they sing the word "jump" and have them shout the word "shout." When they sing the word "praise," have children raise their hands in the air and wave their arms.

Sing the song several times. Start out slowly. Each time you repeat the song, sing it faster.

Say: **Songs are a great way to make a joyful noise to God. Next, let's pray an out-loud prayer of praise.**

9 **Responding to God with prayer**—Have children form a line. Have the first child in line begin the prayer by thanking God for something at church, such as hymns, the Bible, Christian friends, snacks, or the cross in front of the church.

Have the rest of the children repeat in unison what the first child said. When that child is finished, he or she runs to the end of the line. The second child becomes the new leader, who then calls out one more thing to thank God for. The rest of the children quickly repeat it. Encourage the children to move quickly so there's a continuous stream of praise words to God.

Continue until every child has led the prayer at least once.

End the prayer with "Hooray! Amen!"

10 **Responding to God with the closing**—Say: **There are lots of ways to praise God. Today we talked about joyful noises.**

We can be noisy or we can be quiet when we praise God with joyful noises. Our noises can be words, songs, or just silly noises. Let's praise God with silly noises right now.

Give each child a scoop of confetti to hold in both hands. Have children stand in a close circle. Ask one child to make a joyful noise—such as a giggle or a "tra-la-la" or a made-up word—while throwing one handful of confetti into the air. Continue until every child has participated. End with all the children throwing the confetti from their other hands and saying, "We celebrate you, God!"

WORSHIP SERVICE 4

THE DROOPIES

Theme: Sadness

Scriptures: John 11:17-35 and Isaiah 61:1-3

Preparation: You'll need a paper cup for each child and access to water, a Bible, a sheet of newsprint, a marker, crayons, masking tape, and a sheet of white paper.

In this worship service, the children will experience God's care and love for them when they're sad. Often children feel guilty for feeling sad, but in this service, the children will see that sadness is an emotion that everyone shares—even Jesus was sad. They'll learn that God and their friends are waiting to help and comfort them during their saddest moments.

THE SERVICE

1 **Responding to God with creative movement**—Begin the service with this creative movement. Encourage children to follow your actions.

Say: **God, I know I should jump** (jump) **for joy and praise you.** (Wave hands in the air.)

But sometimes I feel so sad, so sad, so sad. (Drop your hands, bow your head, and droop lower each time you say, "so sad.")

God, I know I should twirl (twirl around with arms extended) **because of all the wonderful gifts you give me.**

But sometimes I feel so sad, so sad, so sad. (Drop your hands, bow your head, and droop lower each time you say, "so sad.")

At church, we sing for joy (sing one verse of a praise song, such as "Down in My Heart"),

But sometimes I feel so sad, so sad, so sad. (Drop your hands, bow your head, and droop lower each time you say, "so sad.")

I know you made wonderful colors such as red (point to something red in the room), **blue** (point to something blue in the room), **and yellow** (point to something yellow in the room), **and I should thank you.** (Shout, "Thank you.")

But sometimes I feel so sad, so sad, so sad. (Drop your hands, bow your head, and droop lower each time you say, "so sad.")

Sometimes I feel so sad, so sad, so sad. (Drop your hands, bow your head, and droop lower each time you say, "so sad.")

Have the children sit down. Say: **Sometimes we feel sad, lonely, or scared. We want to talk to God, but sometimes God seems far away. It's hard when we can't see God. So let's sing a song to tell God how we feel.**

2 **Responding to God with music**—Sing "Kumbaya" after you explain that "Kumbaya" means "come by here." Sing the first verse of "Kumbaya" and then use the following words for subsequent verses. Have the children follow your lead as you do the motions in parentheses.

I feel lonely, God; be with me. (Fold your arms across your chest when you sing, "I feel lonely, God." Reach out your hands when you sing, "be with," and point one finger to your chest when you sing "me.")

I feel droopy, God; hear my prayer. (Bow your head when you sing, "I feel droopy, God." Hold your hand to your ear when you sing, "hear my" and fold your hands for "prayer.")

I feel sad today; comfort me. (Make a sad face when you sing, "I feel sad today." Give a child a hug when you sing, "comfort me.")

Oh, Lord, Kumbaya. (Point to heaven. Then roll your forearms from way above your head in toward your body to indicate God coming from heaven.)

Pray: **God, we sing to you when we're happy and also when we're sad. We sing to ask you to be with us all the time. Amen.**

Say: **Now listen to this Bible story about a time Jesus was sad.**

3 **Responding to God with Scripture**—Have the children sit quietly while you read aloud John 11:17-35.

Give each child a small paper cup full of water. Have children walk around the room. When you ask, "What's sad?" have the children pair up with someone close to them. Have partners ask each other what makes them sad.

After each child shares, the partner dips his or her finger into the water and puts a small tear on the other child's cheek. The child then dips his or her finger into the water again and puts a small tear on his or her own cheek while saying, "That's sad. That makes me sad, too." That child then says something that makes him or her sad, and the other child does the motions with the water. Encourage children not to throw water on each other. Remind them this is a worship experience.

Then have the children walk around again until you ask, "What's sad?" Repeat the activity several times. Be sure children pair up with a different child each time. Then ask:

● **How do you feel when sad things happen to your friends?**

● **How does it make you feel when your friends are sad with you?**

Say: **Friends can comfort us when we're feeling sad. God is our very best friend, and God wants to comfort us. Let's talk to God about our sadness now.**

4 **Responding to God with prayer**—Stand with the children in a circle and join hands. Have children follow your actions as you pray:

God, we come to you, and we lift our hands in gratitude for everything you have done. Lift your clasped hands together above your head.

But sometimes we feel sad. Put your arms down and place your head on your right hand, which is still holding someone else's hand.

We're sad sometimes about what happens in our families, but, God, you are always there. We lift our heads toward heaven and smile for everything you have done for us. Look to the sky and smile.

But sometimes we are sad. Put your head down and frown.

We're sad about bad days at school. But we have good days, too. And for those days we clap, jump, and shout "hooray!" Clap, jump, and shout "hooray!"

Thank you for being with us when we're sad. Frown with your head bent down.

And when we're happy. Lift your head and smile.

Say: **This is the good news: God is always with us—even when we're sad. On bad days, we talk to God about how bad we feel. And God always comforts us. On good days, we stop and smile. God is good, and God is always there.**

5 **Responding to God with creative movement**—Have children spread out around the room.

Say: **We sometimes feel alone when we're sad because we don't tell God or other people why we're sad. I'm going to name some things that make people sad, then I'll say a number. If I say "zero," don't talk to anyone. If I say "one," tell one person how you feel about the situation I've named. Whatever number you hear me say, tell that many people how you feel.**

Name situations such as these:

● **Someone calls me names. Zero.**

● **No one will play with me. Two.**

● **Someone yells at me. One.**

● **I feel sick. Zero.**

- **I lost my favorite toy. Two.**
- **I don't want to go to bed. Zero.**
- **My pet is hurt. One.**

Then have the children sit down. Ask:

- **What was it like not to tell anyone about what made you sad?**
- **How did you feel when you told others about your feelings?**

Say: **When we talk to others about the things that make us sad, we often feel better because other people comfort us. Sometimes other people can even help us solve the problems that are making us sad. Let's learn more from the Bible about what we can do when we're sad.**

6 Message—Read aloud Isaiah 61:1-3. Then have the children brainstorm ways to help when other people feel sad. Write the ideas on a sheet of newsprint.

If children have trouble thinking of ideas, ask them how they wish others would help them when they feel sad.

Say: **One way we can help others when they're sad is to give hugs. Let's make each other feel better with big hugs.**

Have the children walk around the room. Have each child take a turn calling out, "I'm sad!" When that happens, all the other children should hurry to give that child a group hug. When everyone has been hugged, have the children sit down.

Say: **Hugs make everyone feel good. Let's give our gifts to God as a way of thanking God for giving us friends who help us feel better when we're sad.**

7 Responding to God by giving—Have children stand in a circle surrounding an offering plate. Say: **Sometimes we don't have money to give as an offering, and that makes us sad. But God also wants us to give God our talents and abilities. We can give to God when we use our talents to serve God.**

Have each child name one talent he or she can give to God and pretend to put it in the offering plate. Then have children put their money offerings in the plate.

Pray: **God, we ask you to use our gifts and our money to help people turn their sadness into gladness by knowing about your love. Amen.**

Say: **Let's sing a song about sadness and gladness.**

8 Responding to God with music—Have children sing these words to the tune of "Row, Row, Row Your Boat":

**God, God, God helps us
When we're sad and blue.
Be with us. Be with us.
Our gladness comes from you.**

The second time through, lead the children in these actions: Raise your arms as you sing "God" in the first line. When you sing the second line, pretend to cry. When you sing the third line, hug yourself. Then, when you sing the fourth line, lift your head to the sky, open your arms, and smile.

Say: **God is happy when we share our sad times and our happy times with God. Let's create pictures about happiness and sadness, and then we'll talk to God.**

9 **Responding to God with prayer**—Post a sheet of newsprint. Draw a horizontal line across the middle of the paper. Using crayons, have each child draw a picture of sadness below the line and a picture of happiness above the line.

After children finish, have everyone hold hands and face the drawing. Start the prayer by saying: God, sometimes we're sad. Have children take turns explaining their picture of sadness. Then have children each explain their pictures of happiness. Say: **God, thank you that our sadness doesn't stay forever. We know you're happy when we're happy. End with a group "amen."**

10 **Responding to God with the closing**—Say: **Let's promise to help each other.**

Write each child's name on a slip of paper and put the papers in a box. Have children spread out around the room. Draw two names out of the box. Have the child whose name was first called skip to the second child and say, "When you're sad, I can be your friend." Call out a third name and have the first two children skip together to the third child, hold hands with that child, and say, "When you're sad, we can be your friends." Continue drawing names until everyone is holding hands.

Then close with this prayer: **Thank you, God, for being there when we're sad. Help us talk to you about what makes us sad. Help us talk to others about what's bothering us. And help us listen when others feel sad. Amen.**

WORSHIP SERVICE 5

THANK YOU, THANK YOU

Theme: Thanksgiving

Scriptures: 1 Thessalonians 5:18 and 2 Corinthians 9:10-15

Preparation: You'll need an inflated balloon for every 10 children; a ball of string and scissors; a large square box; a black marker; tape; an item to toss, such as a small ball or bean bag; and a bowl of small candies.

THE SERVICE

1 Responding to God with creative movement—Before children arrive, cut enough 2-foot-long pieces of string for each child to have one. Make several extras, too. Hide the strings in different places around the room.

When children arrive, have them look for the string. After all the children have found a piece of string, have children tie the pieces together to make one long string. As each child ties his or her string to the others, have him or her say aloud one thing to thank God for. When all the pieces have been tied together, ask:

● **If we thanked God for everything there is to thank God for, how long would our string be?**

● **Why is it good to thank God?**

Say: **God is good. God gives us good gifts. God takes care of us, and God loves us. These are all great reasons to be thankful. Let's sing to God right now.**

2 Responding to God with music—Sing these words to the tune of "London Bridge":

**Thank you, God, for everything:
The warm sun,
Clouds so high.**

Thank you, God, for everything.
You're terrific!

The second time through, lead the children in these motions:

Thank you, God, for everything (twirl around while pointing)**:**
The warm sun (hold hands over head like a sun)**,**
Clouds so high. (Point to various places in the sky as if pointing to different clouds.)
Thank you, God, for everything. (Twirl around while pointing.)
You're terrific. (Jump up.)

The next several times through, have children come up with their own reasons to thank God. Replace the words "the warm sun" and "clouds so high" with the children's reasons.

Say: **God is pleased when we appreciate God. Now let's see what God's Word says.**

3 Responding to God with Scripture—Have the children sit on the floor. Read aloud 1 Thessalonians 5:18. Say: **God knows that there are things we can be thankful for no matter what. It's easy to do that on good days, but even on bad days we can find something to thank God about.**

Have the children form pairs. Have one partner think of something bad that has happened. Have the other partner respond with something to be thankful for even though something bad has happened. For example, one child might say, "It snowed two feet Wednesday night, so my birthday party at school was canceled." The other child might respond, "But we can be thankful that school was called off, too, and we spent the day sledding."

Then have the partners change roles. After they play the game for several minutes, bring the group back together and have volunteers share their ideas with the rest of the class. Then ask:

● **What did you discover about being thankful?**
● **When can you be thankful?**
● **What can you be thankful for?**

Say: **No matter how bad things get or how good things are, we can always be thankful that God loves us and cares for us. Let's talk to God right now.**

4 Responding to God with prayer—Form groups of no more than 10 children each. Give each group a balloon. Say: **Bat or throw the balloon up in the air as high and hard as you can. Then, while the balloon is floating down, tell God what you're thankful for. You'll have to talk fast to name several things because when the balloon lands on the floor, it's the next child's turn.**

Have the groups form circles and pass the balloon around. Play until everyone has at least one turn. Then gather the balloons and all the children in one large group. Toss all the balloons overhead and have the children bat the balloons around while they say, "Thank you, God, for all your gifts. Amen."

Say: **There are so many things to be thankful for that I'm sure we haven't named them all. Let's play a game to help us think of more reasons to be thankful.**

5 **Responding to God with creative movement**—Before class, tape a large square box shut. Using a black marker, make large dots on each side so the box looks like a large die. Vary the number of dots on each side—one side gets one dot, another side gets two dots, and so on.

During class gather the children in a large circle. Call out a category such as colors, animals, foods, places, or hobbies. Have a child roll the die. (Older children may need to help young children.) When the die lands, the child who rolled it names as many things in that category as the number rolled on the die. For example, if a child rolls three and the category is colors, the child could say, "Pink, red, and yellow." Then it's the next child's turn.

Continue until every child has rolled the die at least once. Then put the die away and say: **The world is full of things to be thankful for. Let's learn more about thankfulness from God's Word.**

6 **Message**—Have the children sit quietly in a circle while you read aloud 2 Corinthians 9:10-15.

Then give a small object to one person to toss, such as a beanbag or a small ball. Have that child start a story about thankfulness that fits with the theme of the Scripture. For example, a child might say, "Once upon a time there was a farmer, and he was thankful for the warm sun that allowed his seeds to grow." After a few sentences, have the child throw the object to another child in the circle. Have that child add a few sentences to the story—keeping thankfulness as the main theme. Continue the story until all the children have contributed at least once (or until you get to a good ending).

If the story comes to a natural conclusion before everyone has contributed, start a new story. When you're finished, ask:

● **Why does God give us so much?**

Then say: **We've spent this entire session being thankful, but I know there are other methods to show how thankful we are.**

Ask:

● **What can we do to show our thankfulness?**

If no one mentions "sharing with others," say: **Listen while I read one of the verses again. It mentions another way we can show our thankfulness.** Read 2 Corinthians 9:11. Ask:

● **What does this verse say we can do to show thankfulness?**

Say: **Let's share freely right now.**

7 **Responding to God by giving**—Say: **Because God shares with us, we share with others. To remind us that we give to both God and each other, let's make our offerings with a friend.**

For the offering, form pairs. Have partners put an offering coin between their elbows and then walk together to drop it in the offering plate.

If the children drop a coin along the way, have them pick it up and start again. Have pairs continue doing this until they have given all of their offerings. Be sure to bring extra coins to give to children who don't have offerings.

8 **Responding to God with music**—Say: **God has given us wonderful bodies. Let's use our miraculous bodies to give thanks to God.**

Have children stand in a circle and take turns selecting a creative sound that they can use as a musical instrument, such as clicking their tongues, smacking their lips, humming, scratching their heads, beeping, knocking their knees, whistling, or skipping.

Continue around the circle until every child has thought of a noise. Then lead children as they "sing" "God Is So Good," using their new instruments.

Say: **God *is* so good. Let's thank God in prayer.**

9 **Responding to God with prayer**—Have the children take turns naming things in the room that they are thankful for. Once something has been named, have everyone touch that item.

For example, if a child says, "I'm thankful for brown hair," have the children all touch someone's brown hair. Or if a child says, "I'm thankful for red," have children find and touch something red, such as a red apple on the bulletin board. If a child says, "I'm thankful for Sue," have children run to touch Sue.

Go around the circle several times, giving each child a chance to name one thing when it's his or her turn.

End by saying, **We're thankful for Jesus.** If you have a picture of Jesus, have the children touch it. They could also point to heaven or point to their hearts.

10 **Responding to God with the closing**—Have children sit in a circle. Pass around a bowl of small candies such as M&M's. Have each child take a candy out of the bowl and mention one thing that he or she is thankful for.

Continue passing the bowl until everyone has several candies. Make sure that some candy remains in the bowl, though.

Say: **Each of these candies represents the gifts that God has given us.** Ask:

● **How is candy like the gifts God gives us?**

Hold up the bowl of candy and say: **Even though we each have** received many things, God always has more to give. The Bible says that God will give us everything we need. God has enough for everyone. And God's gifts are always good—even better than this candy. Let's eat our candy as a way of saying thank you to God.

Have children eat the candy. Then have them say together, "Thank you, God, for your wonderful gifts. Amen!"

INDEX

SCRIPTURE INDEX

INDEX

THEME INDEX

Evaluation of *101 Creative Worship Ideas for Children's Church*

Please help Group Publishing, Inc., continue providing innovative and usable resources for ministry by taking a moment to fill out and send us this evaluation. Thanks!

● ● ●

1. As a whole, this book has been (circle one)

Not much help   Very helpful

1   2   3   4   5   6   7   8   9   10

2. The things I liked best about this book were:

3. This book could be improved by:

4. One thing I'll do differently because of this book is:

5. Optional Information:

Name_____

Street Address _____

City_____ State _____Zip _____

Phone Number _____Date _____

Group's
Hands-On
BIBLE
CURRICULUM

TEACH YOUR PRESCHOOLERS AS JESUS TAUGHT WITH GROUP'S *HANDS-ON BIBLE CURRICULUM*™

Hands-On Bible Curriculum™ for preschoolers helps your preschoolers learn the way they learn best—by touching, exploring, and discovering. With active learning, preschoolers love learning about the Bible, and they really remember what they learn.

Because small children learn best through repetition, Preschoolers and Pre-K & K will learn one important point per lesson, and Toddlers & 2s will learn one point each month with **Hands-On Bible Curriculum**. These important lessons will stick with them and comfort them during their daily lives. Your children will learn:

- •God is our friend,
- •who Jesus is, and
- •we can always trust Jesus.

The **Learning Lab®** is packed with age-appropriate learning tools for fun, faith-building lessons. Toddlers & 2s explore big **Interactive StoryBoards™** with enticing textures that toddlers love to touch. **Bible Big Books™** captivate Preschoolers and Pre-K & K while teaching them important Bible lessons. With **Jumbo Bible Puzzles™** and involving **Learning Mats™**, your children will see, touch, and explore their Bible stories. Each quarter there's a brand new collection of supplies to keep your lessons fresh and involving.

Fuzzy, age-appropriate hand puppets are also available to add to the learning experience. These child-friendly puppets help you teach each lesson with scripts provided in the **Teachers Guide**. Cuddles the Lamb, Whiskers the Mouse, and Pockets the Kangaroo turn each lesson into an interactive and entertaining learning experience.

Just order one **Learning Lab** and one **Teachers Guide** for each age level, add a few common classroom supplies, and presto—you have everything you need to build faith in your children. For more interactive fun, introduce your children to the age-appropriate puppet who will be your teaching assistant and their friend. **No student books required!**

Hands-On Bible Curriculum is also available for grades 1–6.

Order today from your local Christian bookstore, or write: Group Publishing, Box 485, Loveland, CO 80539.

MORE INNOVATIVE RESOURCES
FOR YOUR YOUTH MINISTRY

The Youth Worker's Encyclopedia of Bible-Teaching Ideas:
Old Testament/ New Testament

Explore the most comprehensive idea-books available for youth workers! Discover more than 360 creative ideas in each encyclopedia—there's at least one idea for each and every book of the Bible. Find ideas for...retreats and overnighters, learning games, adventures, special projects, parties, prayers, music, devotions, skits, and much more!

Plus, you can use these ideas for groups of all sizes in any setting. Discover exciting new ways to teach each book of the Bible to your youth group.

Old Testament	ISBN 1-55945-184-X
New Testament	ISBN 1-55945-183-1

Clip-Art Cartoons for Churches

Here are over 180 funny, photocopiable illustrations to help you jazz up your calendars, newsletters, posters, fliers, transparencies, postcards, business cards, announcements—all your printed materials! These fun, fresh illustrations cover a variety of church and Christian themes, including church life, Sunday school, youth groups, school life, sermons, church events, volunteers, and more!

Each illustration is provided in the sizes you need most, so it's easy to use. Order your copy of **Clip-Art Cartoons for Churches** today...and add some spice to your next printed piece.

ISBN 1-55945-791-0

Bore No More! (For Every Pastor, Speaker, Teacher)

This book is a must for every pastor, youth leader, teacher, and speaker. These 70 audience-grabbing activities pull listeners into your lesson or sermon—and drive your message home!

Discover clever object lessons, creative skits, and readings. Music and celebration ideas. Affirmation activities. All the innovative techniques 85 percent of adult churchgoers say they wish their pastors would try! (recent Group Publishing poll)

Involve your congregation in the learning process! Order today! ISBN 1-55945-266-8